ROUTLEDGE LIBRARY EDITIONS: POLICE AND POLICING

Volume 13

POLICE AND GOVERNMENT

POLICE AND GOVERNMENT

The Status and Accountability of the English Constable

GEOFFREY MARSHALL

Routledge
Taylor & Francis Group

LONDON AND NEW YORK

First published in 1965 by Methuen & Co Ltd

This edition first published in 2023
by Routledge
4 Park Square, Milton Park, Abingdon, Oxon OX14 4RN

and by Routledge
605 Third Avenue, New York, NY 10158

*Routledge is an imprint of the Taylor & Francis Group, an
informa business*

British Library Cataloguing in Publication Data
A catalogue record for this book is available from the British
Library

ISBN: 978-1-032-41114-9 (Set)
ISBN: 978-1-032-41937-4 (Volume 13) (hbk)
ISBN: 978-1-032-41940-4 (Volume 13) (pbk)
ISBN: 978-1-003-36049-0 (Volume 13) (ebk)

DOI: 10.4324/9781003360490

Publisher's Note
The publisher has gone to great lengths to ensure the quality
of this reprint but points out that some imperfections in the
original copies may be apparent.

Disclaimer
The publisher has made every effort to trace copyright
holders and would welcome correspondence from those they
have been unable to trace.

Police and Government

The Status and Accountability of the English Constable

GEOFFREY MARSHALL

METHUEN & CO LTD *11 New Fetter Lane London EC4*

First published in Great Britain in 1965
© 1965 by Geoffrey Marshall
Printed in Great Britain by
Butler & Tanner Ltd
Frome and London

*'The history of the police
is the history of
the office of constable'*
HALSBURY, *Laws of England*

Contents

Preface

POLICE, IN A DEMOCRACY, IS A DELICATE, OFTEN DANGEROUS function and the United Kingdom has been honestly served in it. That is a primary acknowledgment to be made at the outset of any discussion of police responsibilities. It is, I hope, unneccessary to suggest that although in this essay I have attacked a well-known theory about police independence which many policemen would wish to defend, the argument advanced is not in any sense an argument either 'for' or 'against' the police. I assume without question that the interest of the police in clarifying the issue of their constitutional status and accountability is identical with that of the rest of society and the assumption is one which I have always found police officers to share.

I should like to acknowledge my indebtedness for information and assistance of various kinds to the following: Professor Bryan Keith-Lucas; Mr K. P. Poole of the Association of Municipal Corporations; Mr D. N. Chester, Warden of Nuffield College Oxford; Mr Harry Plowman, Town Clerk of Oxford; Professor R. C. Cross; Mr L. H. Hoffman; Mrs Jenifer Hart; and Mr P. J. Stead. None of them is to be associated, of course, with any opinions here expressed.

Acknowledgment is also due to the Editors of *Public Law*, *Public Administration* and *The Guardian* for permission to make use of material originally appearing in those journals, and to H.M.S.O. and the Association of Municipal Corporations for permission to reprint the extracts included in the Appendices.

I am grateful to Mr Richard Oakley for compiling the index.

1 Police Accountability: The Problem

WHAT IS THE PRECISE CONSTITUTIONAL STATUS OF THE British police constable? It should, perhaps, be a matter for surprise that in the second half of the twentieth century the answer to this question remains ambiguous. Little in fact has been written about it in the standard textbooks on central and local government or in constitutional commentaries. But since the late 1950s, increasing attention has been focused on police activities and what was once merely a neglected theoretical issue is now a question of some practical and political importance. In the 1930s, it is true, problems of public order, largely caused by Fascist and anti-Fascist gatherings, raised questions about police accountability and brought to notice the difficulties involved in discussing the provincial police both in the House of Commons and in local council chambers. But more urgent matters between 1939 and 1945 removed the desire or possibility of any general inquiry into the problems thrown up by pre-war experience and it was not until a decade later that attention returned to them, partly again, perhaps, because of police activity in controlling political demonstrations of various flavours and partly because of an increasing traffic problem bringing more people of all social classes into contact with the police. The increasingly sensitive attention paid to problems of public administration and maladministration by the popular press and by television may also have played a part.

In 1959 there was set up a Royal Commission on the Police. Though there had been earlier Commissions and Committees on police powers and other aspects of police service, this was the first comprehensive attempt to review the status, organization and accountability of the twentieth-century police. The reasons for holding such an inquiry multiplied during the 1950s. Between 1956 and 1960 in particular an unusual crop of incidents drew the public eye to police affairs. Disciplinary action or legal proceedings were instituted against the chief constables of three forces – Cardiganshire, Worcester and Brighton. There were parliamentary debates and a tribunal of inquiry into the behaviour of two members of the Thurso police and there was a censure motion in the House of Commons after an alleged assault by a metropolitan policeman had led to a Home Office settlement of the resulting action. In the 1960s allegations about and investigations into police behaviour have followed each other with percussive regularity. But the affair which most directly raised the question of the status and accountability of the police was a prolonged disagreement in Nottingham in 1959 between the watch committee as police authority and the chief constable, Captain Athelstan Popkess.

The Nottingham case brought about – possibly for the first time – a debate of a detailed character about the exact constitutional relationship between local police authorities and the police acting as law enforcement officers. The Home Office, which secured the reinstatement of Captain Popkess after his suspension by the watch committee, took the view that chief officers of police, as constables at common law, exercise a discretionary authority in keeping the peace and are not subject to control or instructions by watch committees whilst performing their law enforcement functions. This generalization about the status of constables derives its force largely from a well-known decision *Fisher v. Oldham Corporation*.[1] Yet on the face of it such a view appeared to many local authority representatives to derogate from the statutory responsibility placed upon local authorities for the efficient policing of their areas and they were reluctant to concede that no legal powers existed to control the enforcement of the law and the operations of the police. Obvious uncertainties were revealed as to the boundaries of their authority and as to the interpretation to be placed upon the notion of 'law enforcement'. In the

[1] [1930] 2 K.B. 364. See below, Chap. 3.

aftermath of the Nottingham case a number of queries were posed. In a discussion for example in 1960 in the journal *Public Administration*,[1] Mr D. N. Chester, Warden of Nuffield College, Oxford, pointed to some of the difficulties inherent in the idea of 'enforcement'. Most people he suggested were thinking, in using the term 'law enforcement', of particular offences such as housebreaking, where offenders are detected and the law takes its course. Here no borough councillor or watch committee would regard themselves as having the right to interfere or to pass resolutions instructing a chief constable not to enforce certain branches of the law. This would be equivalent to the borough contracting out of the general law. But he added:

> . . . consider three possible sets of circumstances. First: a town in which organized gangs of youths are fighting among themselves and terrorizing peaceful citizens; second: a town in which political demonstrations are taking place and feeling running high; third: a town in which the citizens are greatly concerned about the number of people killed and injured in the area by motor vehicles.

Would it be out of order in the first instance, he asked, if the chairman of the watch committee were to be asked by a councillor what measures the police were taking? Would the chairman be correct if he replied that this was not a matter for the council but a matter of law enforcement and therefore a matter solely for the chief constable? Could not the council pass a resolution urging more vigorous action and legitimately dismiss the chief constable if they were satisfied that the resolution had not been obeyed? In the second instance would the watch committee be legally helpless if the police had used unnecessary force in controlling demonstrations? Would it be *ultra vires* for the watch committee to instruct the chief constable to order his force to use gentler methods in future? In the third case might the police authority instruct the chief constable to make more efforts to catch and charge motorists exceeding the speed limit? Might there not indeed have been a tendency in recent years to emphasize the

[1] See B. Keith-Lucas and D. N. Chester, 'The Independence of Chief Constables', *Public Administration*, 1960, p. 1; G. Marshall, 'Police Responsibility', *Public Administration*, 1960, p. 213.

independence of the chief constable and to reduce the responsibility of the police authority? If the police were as independent as had been argued, in what sense could it be said that police was a local authority function?[1]

It seems odd perhaps that with so much room for divergences of view about the powers of police and watch committees, disputes have not been more frequent. Before 1959 the only documented case of any seriousness seems to have been the disagreement between the chief constable and watch committee of St Helens in the 1920s. That, however, did not turn upon any high constitutional points but on a series of petty squabbles and mutual accusations of discourtesy and dishonesty terminating in 1927 in an unscrupulous attempt by the watch committee to dismiss the chief constable by a form of proceeding under which it was thought that he would have no right of appeal. The story can be read in the reports of the inquiries[2] set up by the Home Office, one of them being a successful appeal by the chief constable against his dismissal. The only matter of general interest amongst the many points of disagreement was perhaps one which arose from the use to be made in 1926 of police drafted into St Helens at the time of the general strike. The disposition of these extra police was evidently discussed by the watch committee and there was some disagreement both within the committee and with the chief constable as to whether the imported men should be used in the mining parts of St Helens or on the ordinary street beats. The report however does not suggest that it was in any way improper for such issues to be dealt with by the watch committee or that the chief constable made any demur as to their rights in the matter. It was simply another episode in a series of personal animosities and misunderstandings. Another followed when the force was paraded to be addressed on the necessity for discretion and avoidance of violence. They were to be admonished on this topic by the chief constable and the chairman and vice-chairman of the watch committee. An 'angry altercation' then arose when further members of the watch committee arrived with the intention of making speeches.

[1] *Ibid.*, at pp. 12-15.
[2] Both reports are printed in Cmd. 3103 (1928).

Recriminations continued in which it was alleged that one councillor had been described by the chief constable as a 'liar and a
twister' and that the councillor had replied that the chief constable
was himself 'the biggest liar and twister in St Helens'.[1] In this vein
matters continued until the committee's final attempt at dismissal
which arose from an equally trivial episode of alleged discourtesy.

No sensible general conclusions could be drawn from the St
Helens case about either watch committees or chief constables. The
facts of the Nottingham case in 1959, however, are of greater significance since they turned upon the rights of the watch committee
to require reports on matters of law enforcement. The issue nevertheless involved a type of conflict between the police authority and
its chief constable of a rather special kind which is unlikely to occur
with any frequency, in that the matters on which the chief constable
was asked to report involved members of the authority themselves.
Captain Popkess, the chief constable, had instituted inquiries, after
consultation with the Director of Public Prosecutions, into various
matters affecting members of the council, including the claiming of
expenses and the carrying out of certain work by the corporation.
The Town Clerk and the watch committee took exception to the
manner in which the inquiries had been conducted and asked for a
report from the chief constable. This Captain Popkess refused to
give on the ground that the responsibility for law enforcement was
his and that it was not a matter with which the watch committee
might properly concern itself. The watch committee thereupon sus-
pended him from duty in the exercise of their powers under s. 191
of the Municipal Corporations Act, 1882, until such time as they
should have considered the matter further. Meanwhile the Home
Office asked for confirmation and an explanation of the grounds for
suspension. The Home Secretary in a parliamentary written reply[2]
on 16 July 1959 stated that the watch committee's principal
grounds were the refusal of the chief constable to comply with the
committee's instructions to inform them about inquiries by Scotland Yard officers into corporation matters in Nottingham and the

---

[1] *Op. cit.*, p. 8.
[2] 609 H.C. Deb. 5s. col. 52.

report of the Town Clerk about the chief constable's conduct. At a meeting in the Home Office the Town Clerk explained that his report related to two cases in which police inquiries were made affecting members or officers of the council which were carried out in circumstances which he considered to have disclosed a lack of impartiality on the chief constable's part.

The Home Secretary stated that he had written to the Nottingham watch committee informing them that he did not consider that the circumstances justified the suspension. He had told them that in his view the chief constable would have been in breach of his duty if he had complied with the instruction; that a chief officer of police had a duty to enforce the criminal law and that he should not in doing so be subject to control or interference by the police authority. Upon this the watch committee reinstated Captain Popkess, pending his retirement at the end of the year, stating that they did so reluctantly.

The Nottingham episode was not perhaps an entirely typical example of the difficulty of principle which may arise from the unresolved rights of police authorities in matters which verge on the sphere of law enforcement. From the circumstances of the case and the Home Office's attitude it was not easy to infer any concise conclusion. Did the Home Office think that all requests for reports on operational matters constituted an 'interference' with law enforcement? Or was the Nottingham action improper because it was an instruction rather than a request? Or because it involved particular cases rather than general policy? Or because it involved possible prosecutions as distinct from other police operations and dispositions? These were the questions to which clear and consistent answers seemed to be needed. It might have been supposed, after a Royal Commission and a comprehensive revision of police legislation, that clear and consistent answers would have emerged. But that, unfortunately, cannot be said.

2 The Office of Constable

THE CRUX OF THE CONSTITUTIONAL ISSUE IS THE RELATION between police and police authority. In the statutory organization of the nineteenth and twentieth centuries there have been three types of police authority. In England and Wales the function was given to watch committees in the boroughs and to standing joint committees of county councillors and justices in county areas. In Scotland the council itself was made the police authority in both counties and burghs. In the metropolitan area the Home Secretary is the police authority. The Home Secretary has also in some sense a responsibility for law and order throughout the country. He has statutory power to frame certain types of regulation for the administration of police forces, to act as an appeal authority in disciplinary matters and to approve the appointment of chief constables.[1] Fifty per cent of approved local authority expenditure on police comes from an exchequer grant which is conditional *inter alia* on the Secretary of State's being satisfied that the area in question is efficiently policed. For this purpose a force of inspectors is maintained.

Such are the outline facts about police authorities.[2] But what is a police authority? To this question the statutes give some answers but

---

[1] Additional powers conferred by the Police Act, 1964, are considered in Chap. 7.

[2] A full description of police organization is to be found in a number of places, the most useful being Halsbury, *Laws of England*, 3rd ed., Vol. 30, pp. 43–145; Jenifer Hart, *The British Police*; and *Royal Commission on the Police*, 1962, *Final Report*, Cmnd. 1728, Chap. 3. On Scotland, *Memorandum of the Scottish Home Department* (Cmd. 1728, Minutes of Evidence, Appendix II, pp. 39–87). J. D. B. Mitchell, 'The Constitutional Position of the Police in Scotland', 1962, *Juridical Review*, 1, and *Encyclopedia of the Laws of Scotland*, Vol. 11, pp. 376–416.

not all of them. A full description of the function depends in part upon what the common law, rightly considered, has to say about the nature of constabulary functions. For, it is said, 'in essence a police force is neither more nor less than a number of individual constables whose status derives from the common law, organized together in the interests of efficiency'.[1] It is by the appointment of constables that localities are to be policed. But what is a constable? To this question the textbooks supply some striking and perhaps puzzling answers. He is, it has been suggested, a 'servant of the state' and 'a ministerial officer of the central power'. He holds office under Her Majesty. But he is not quite, it seems, a servant of Her Majesty or of the Crown. Outside the metropolis he is employed by a local authority who appoint him, and until 1964 might dismiss him. Yet he is not, so we may read, the servant of his police authority and is in no way answerable to them for the manner in which he keeps the peace. His powers are 'original, not delegated'. They are exercised by him in virtue of his office, and unless he is acting in execution of a warrant lawfully issued, they can only be exercised on his own responsibility.[2] When he exercises them no Minister is directly responsible to Parliament for the results in quite the same manner as for other executive officers.

All this adds up to a curious theory. The implications which have been drawn from it ascribe to police officers an independence and freedom from control unique amongst officials exercising executive functions. These inferences are, however, fairly modern ones. Indeed it might be said that they have only really crystallized since 1930. How, we must ask, did they come to be accepted?

Some part of the explanation may lie in the vagueness or ambiguity of the language traditionally used to describe police functions in Britain. Words such as 'original' and 'independent', for example, offer at least the possibility of a running together of the ideas of independent historical origin and present freedom from subordination. Adding to the confusion is another class of traditional statements about the British police which sound at first hearing contradictory but in which it is not always easy to detect the existence of any

[1] Halsbury, *Laws of England*, 3rd ed., Vol. 30, p. 43.   [2] *Ibid.*

meaning at all. One such recently quoted observation asserts that 'The police of this country have never been recognized either in law or by tradition as a force distinct from the general body of citizens'.[1] What can this be intended to imply? That, perhaps, we do not recognize policemen when we see them? Or that we do not distinguish policemen and their functions from those of, say, milkmen or bookmakers? Obviously not this. But then what does it tell us? In some ways it would be true to say that traffic wardens are a force 'distinct from the general body of citizens'. In another sense one might believe that the East German People's Police are not a force distinct from the general body of East German citizens. It depends on the criteria used to distinguish. If it has any force, this, like many proverbial sayings, is at least partially contradicted by the remarks about uniqueness and independence and either view may be invoked according to need and circumstance. In making the case for increased remuneration for the police, for example, the Royal Commission in its interim report of 1960 laid emphasis on the unique duties and responsibilities placed on police officers. In the major report, however, they began by repeating with approval the remark that a police constable is only 'a person paid to perform as a matter of duty acts which if he were so minded he might have done voluntarily'. (This pristine reflection is, in any event, not altogether accurate as a guide to law enforcement in the twentieth century, when statute has clothed the police with a number of powers not shared by citizens at large.)

The step from 'original' to 'discretionary' powers is by no means a logically necessary one; yet the transition has been easily made. The Willink Report speaks of evidence given before the commission which had suggested that 'because his powers are "original" and not "delegated", the constable *therefore* enjoys a degree of independence in the exercise of these powers'.[2] But it cannot follow solely from the historical fact that the powers originate in a particular way or from the legal fact that they are conferred directly by statute, that

[1] Cmnd. 1728, p. 10; quoted from the *Royal Commission on Police Powers and Procedure* of 1929 (Cmd. 3297).

[2] Cmnd. 1728, p. 11 (italics added).

any particular degree of independence from external control now exists. If that conclusion is true it must at least rest upon some argument about the content of the original power, and be conditioned by the rights and duties which other persons and authorities have acquired either from the common law or from Parliament. Nor can it be maintained as the Willink Report suggests that 'This claim to a measure of independence from outside control is reflected in the terms of the declaration made by a constable on appointment'.[1] The form of declaration cited[2] implies that constables hold an office under the Crown and are pledged to preserve the Queen's peace according to law. In itself it neither states nor reflects anything about the specific way in which the peace is to be kept, except that it shall be preserved in a lawful manner. Again, what that manner is must depend upon what the law, rightly interpreted, is. No one would suggest that allegiance to the Crown or service under it in itself entailed any possession of independent discretionary authority or immunity from control. It has never been supposed that there is any difficulty about the subjection of the military and civil services of the Crown to detailed control or instructions by political superiors.

The police, like the military forces of the Crown, are in fact in obvious ways a disciplined force and not a body of atomic individuals each keeping the peace on his own responsibility and in a manner judged best to himself. This fact causes some embarrassment to the traditional doctrine. 'It appears odd,' says the Willink Commission, 'that the constable enjoys a traditional status which implies a degree of independence belied by his subordinate rank in the force.'[3] The Royal Commission of 1929 on Police Powers and Procedure suggested rather obscurely that the grading of police officers

---

[1] *Ibid.*

[2] 'I A.B. do declare that I will well and truly serve our Sovereign Lady the Queen in the office of constable, without favour or affection, malice or ill-will; and that I will to the best of my power cause the peace to be kept and preserved, and prevent all offences against the persons and properties of her Majesty's subjects; and that while I continue to hold the said office I will to the best of my skill and knowledge discharge all the duties thereof faithfully according to law. So help me God.'

[3] Cmnd. 1728, p. 25.

in ranks has 'for the most part only an administrative as distinct from a legal significance' since duties are imposed upon every constable by law and they cannot be widened or restricted by any superior officer or administrative authority'.[1] The distinction between 'administrative' and 'legal' significance is an odd one. It cannot really be suggested that the orders involved in organized police work are just a matter of friendly co-operation between a number of constables. They are after all enforced by a disciplinary code drawn up by authority of Parliament. And what is to be understood by 'widened' or 'restricted'? A constable's duties obviously cannot be restricted in such a way as to involve him in illegal actions but there are numerous ways in which his discretion as to the manner in which he keeps the peace or the occasions on which he charges offenders can be restricted by his superior officers. In fact the Commission state in their next paragraph that the duty of a chief constable is to direct the activities of the members of his force. He is entitled to see that they properly discharge the duties of their office of constable. It cannot easily be denied that he is thereby entitled to direct them, within the bounds of legality, to police the area in such detailed manner as he deems proper and not as they do. Moreover, the Royal Commission did not in 1929 draw the conclusion that the chief officer in right of his office of constable must exercise his judgment independently of the local police authority. They speak of him as directing the activities of the police 'with the approval of his police authority'. They say (at para. 38) that 'The chief constable is responsible to his police authority'. As with the superior officers in the force it is implied that the form of supervision involved is that of ensuring that the members of the force properly discharge the duties of their office.

Within the force organized law enforcement implies that the constable – his original powers and his obligation to the Queen and her Peace notwithstanding – may properly be given orders and instructions as to the times, places and manner in which his duties are to be carried out. Yet no inconsistency seems to have been observed in citing a chief officer's status as a common law constable as in itself

[1] Cmd. 3297 (1929), p. 15.

sufficient to establish that he must be immune from any specific instructions as to the manner in which he carries out the duties of his office. Whatever the theory, individual constables (though they may frequently make arrests on their own initiative and exercise a considerable degree of personal judgment in maintaining order) do not, in charging offenders, act solely upon their own views of law or policy. The same is true of senior officers. The application of the law is neither an automatic process, nor, in its discretionary and public policy aspects, a matter in which chief constables themselves act without guidance or without what even may amount to a form of instruction. The police are not completely free to investigate crime in any manner they please even when their actions are lawful. One example of a restriction in the law enforcement field relates to the tapping of telephones. Though the practice is approved in defined cases it cannot by direction of the Secretary of State be engaged in without a specific authorization in each instance by the Home Office.[1] Another example of centralized restriction is supplied by the detailed 'administrative directions' as to the procedure to be followed in questioning persons suspected of offences, which were circulated by the Home Office with the revised Judges' Rules in 1964. These themselves are in practice a form of instruction to police officers. (The Home Office circular is entitled *Judges' Rules and Administrative Directions to the Police*.[2]) Nor again may the police prosecute at their discretion in every case in which breaches of the law are discovered. There is a large number of statutory provisions[3] which restrict the institution of proceedings without the leave of either the Attorney-General or the Director of Public Prosecutions.

[1] All applications are considered by senior officers in the criminal department of the Home Office and submitted to the Secretary of State. There is a quarterly review of outstanding warrants by the Permanent Under-Secretary. Cmnd. 283 (1957), p. 18.

[2] Circular No. 31/1964. (See Appendix A.) Cf. also the type of circular which the Home Office issued to the Metropolitan Police setting out the way in which the Street Offences Act, 1959, was to be enforced and the manner in which cautions were to be issued by constables acting in pairs. See 604 H.C. Deb. 5s. col. 401.

[3] At least eighty according to the Attorney-General in 1958. (See his evidence to the House of Commons Select Committee on Obscene Publications, H.C. 123-1 (1958) p. 23.) Also J. Ll. J. Edwards, *The Law Officers of the Crown*, p. 237.

Even outside these there may be central initiative or restraint. In July 1964, for example, all chief constables in England and Wales were asked to consult the Director of Public Prosecutions before prosecuting certain forms of homosexual conduct. The existence of such restrictions indicates that 'independence' and 'responsibility only to the law' are not synonymous. For the law and its associated practice may incorporate restrictions in matters of policy, enforcement and investigation. If these cut into the principle that 'in all his police functions a chief officer acts at his own discretion and not under the orders of anybody else', so much the worse, apparently, for the principle.

THE ORIGINAL OFFICE

Despite the weight placed in recent times on the doctrine of individual constabulary independence there seems surprisingly little before 1900 in either the law reports or in the writing of commentators which equates the position of constables with independence of action and freedom from control, though Blackstone certainly thought that their powers of arrest and of entering property were large in relation to their intelligence and character. ('Of the extent of their powers', he wrote, 'considering what manner of men are for the most part put into these offices, it is perhaps very well that they are kept in ignorance'.[1]) The office itself had its origins in military functions representing a 'fusion of popular and royal authority'.[2] Coke, it is agreed, mistakenly attributed the source of the high constable's authority to statute. In *Regina v. Wyatt*, Powell J. is reported as follows: 'My Lord Coke 4 Inst. 267 says that a constable of a hundred was not an officer at common law but created by the Statute of Winchester. . . . But I hold that he was an officer at common law and the Statute of Winchester only enlarged his authority in some particulars.'[3]

The office is also one which, being concerned with the King's peace, is thereby in a certain sense connected with the Crown.

[1] *Commentaries on the Law of England*, Vol. 1, pp. 355–6 (16th ed., 1825).
[2] Helen M. Cam, *The Hundred and the Hundred Rolls* (1930), pp. 188–94.
[3] Ld Raym. 1189.

Mackalley's[1] case reported by Coke shows one purpose for which this was so.

Mackalley's case. The issue arose on an indictment for murder and the facts as set out were these: Richard Fells, a sergeant of the mace in London, had placed one John Murray under arrest. As the report continues:

> It so then and there happened that the said John Murray . . . one John Mackall, late of London, yeoman, otherwise called Mackalley . . . one John Engles . . . and one Archebald Miller . . . not having the fear of God before their eyes but moved and seduced by the instigation of the devil, with force and arms, that is to say with swords etc. to the intent him the said John Murray from his arrest then and there to rescue in and upon the aforesaid Richard Fells then and there made an assault and affray, in which said affray the aforesaid John Mackall otherwise called John Mackalley with a sword called a rapier, made of iron and steel of the value of 12d . . . the said Richard Fells in and upon the left part of his body . . . feloniously, voluntarily and of malice aforethought then and there struck and thrust in, giving to the said Richard Fells . . . one blow and mortal wound of the length of half an inch and of the breadth of half an inch and of the depth of six inches, of which said stroke and mortal wound aforesaid, the aforesaid Richard Fells then and there, that is to say in the parish and ward last aforesaid, instantly died.

The argument in the case raised the questions whether the original arrest was tortious and whether the killing of the sergeant was murder or manslaughter. The judge resolved that it was murder. The killing of any magistrate or minister of justice was a disobedience to the King and to the law, 'and therefore, if a sheriff, justice of the peace, *chief constable, petit constable, watchman or any other minister of the king, or any who comes to their aid,* be killed in doing of their office it is murder'.[2]

From the point of view which interests us, nothing very much about the precise status of constables can be inferred from *Mackalley's* case. The relation to the Crown of the collection of persons mentioned obviously differed in important ways. It was not necessary to

---

[1] Co. Rep. 62b.   [2] At 68a, 68b (italics added).

say anything about the status and powers of any of them, justices, constables or private persons except that for the purpose in hand they were acting for the preservation of the peace and in that sense were acting in the King's name and were 'Ministers of the King'. But apart from this we learn nothing about the duties or immunities of constables[1] any more than of justices, private persons or watchmen.

Nothing which helps to resolve the modern controversy seems to be found in the textbook writers any more than in the law reports. All emphasize the maintenance of the peace and the various actions necessary to that end. William Lambard in 1602 derives the name of the office from words which give a literal flavour to the support rendered to the fountainhead of justice. 'The name constable is made (as I have heard) of two English words put together, namely Cuning (or Cyng) and Staple, which do signify the stay (or hold) of the King'.[2] Besides the direct suppression of disorder there is a preventive function which may be exercised upon 'suspected persons which walk in the night, sleep in the day: or which do haunt any house where is suspicion of baudie' – 'and they may carry them before a Justice of the Peace to find sureties of their good behaviour'. It is added that 'a great part of their duty (concerning the Peace) resteth in the making of due execution of the precepts of higher officers and especially of the Justices of the Peace who be (as it were) immediately set over them'.[3]

---

[1] The appointment of deputies by constables led to some debate about the nature of their functions. 'Of officers there are two kinds,' it was said in *Phelps v. Winchcomb*, 'a judicial officer and a ministerial; a judicial officer cannot make a deputy because he is called to do justice; otherwise it is of a ministerial officer, who may make his deputy.' A constable, the judges thought, might so appoint a deputy. (3 Bulstr. 77, 78.) A similar question was argued in *Midhurst v. Waite* (1761), an action brought by an alehouse keeper against a deputy high constable for billeting soldiers. The plaintiff argued that no judicial officer could appoint a deputy and that a high constable was in some respects a judicial officer. The billeting of soldiers at least was a judicial act. To this Lord Mansfield replied that not every act in which the judgment of the agent was exercised could be termed 'judicial'. This was a ministerial act and a deputy might be appointed to do it. (3 Burr. 1260, 1262.)

[2] *The Duties of Constables, Borsholders, Tythingmen and such other low and lay Ministers of the Peace*, pp. 4–5 ('comes stabuli' – Master of the Horse – is, however, the generally accepted derivation).

[3] Lambard, pp. 12, 19.

Bacon's essay on constables[1] asserts that the office of high constable 'grew in use for the receiving of the commandments and prescripts from the justices of the peace and distributing them to the petty constables'. In Burn's *Justice of the Peace* the greater part of the business of high constables is said to be appropriated to them 'as officers to execute the precepts of the justices of the peace, which any other person may do as well as they'.[2] Blackstone deals fairly briefly with the high and petty constable along with a number of officers, amongst them gaolers, bailiffs and coroners, but nothing in his discussion bears directly upon the question of the propriety of instructions or control of constables in the exercise of their common law powers. Nor do later commentators or historians deal with the question, being mainly concerned with the origins of the office and with various forms of change in its duties and importance.[3] Sir William Holdsworth shows how the importance of the constable tended to increase as statute imposed a miscellany of duties on him. But by the eighteenth century his status had diminished and 'he tended to become merely the servant of the justices'.[4] This is the common refrain. Alongside the common law power to keep the King's peace stands the notion of service to localities and to the local justices. This was so from the earliest times. In an essay on shire officials in the fourteenth century Miss Helen Cam has written that constables 'might in their different capacities have to obey and act with specially appointed military officials like arrayers and *electores peditum*, with the keepers of the peace, with the coroners, with the bailiffs of hundreds and liberties and with the sheriff when he called out the forces of the shire to back up his authority'. For their common law duties 'the responsibility was their own – and arose from the circumstances and they required no mandate from the sheriff to

[1] 'The Office of Constables' (1608), *Works*, Vol. 7 p. 749 (ed. Spedding and Ellis, 1859).

[2] *Op. cit.*, Vol. 2, pp. 539, 545 (21st ed., 1810). Cf. Hawkins, *Pleas of the Crown*, Vol. 2, p. 98 (8th ed., 1824).

[3] H. B. Simpson's article 'The Office of Constable', *English Historical Review*, 1895, is a case in point. Though cited by McCardie J. in *Fisher's* case and elsewhere it is not directed to the constitutional question here in issue. Nor is anything said on the matter in Chitty's *Summary of the Office and Duties of Constables* (3rd ed., 1844).

[4] *History of English Law*, Vol. 10, p. 231. Cf. Vol. 4, p. 125.

authorize their action'.[1] This passage brings out aptly the independence involved in the exercise of common law powers. Such powers allowed constables to act on the authority of their office. Here they could act without need for instructions from sheriffs or justices. But the possession of an independently derived right to act does not in itself entail a general immunity from all supervision in the execution of their duty. In matters of the peace a constable might in fact draw his authority either from the powers of his common law office or from his carrying out of directions properly given him, but there seems no suggestion that there is in some sense a boundary placed around the common law powers which walls them off from lawful instructions by justices or others as to their manner of exercise. No justice and no man could give to any constable (or any citizen) orders which involved him in a violation of the general law of the land, or of his allegiance to the Crown, or in disregard of any specific statutory duty placed upon him. But between the concept of lawful instructions and the exercise of 'original' common law powers, no contradiction, it seems, was thought to arise.

THE EFFECT OF STATUTORY REGULATION

The latter-day theory about the independence of constables may be not unconnected with the retention of a predominantly local system of policing and with the traditional sentiment that independent police forces not subject to national control are a bulwark against continental forms of tyranny. Feelings about the political undesirability of directing constabulary forces from a single administrative centre have perhaps overlapped with the notion that the members of such forces ought to be under no form of external direction at all. If the nineteenth-century statutory regulation of police forces had taken the form of setting up a single national force it seems doubtful whether so much would have been heard about the autonomous common law powers of constables. Such a doctrine would have cut across the necessities of public accountability to Ministers and Parliament. Some influential opinion in fact certainly favoured this Benthamite solution for the whole country after the metropolitan police

[1] Helen M. Cam in *The English Government at Work 1327–1336*, Vol. III, p. 171.

had furnished a model. The commissioners who reported in 1839[1] on the most efficient way of policing the counties were strongly in favour of some form of central responsibility. Their report[2] contains some interesting reflections on the general nature of police duties and a great deal of information about the autonomous peace-keeping activities of local constables and justices.

> In one district, for example, exposed to the offence of sheep stealing, on the occurrence of a theft the constables were directed to enter the cottages of all the labourers in a village before dinner-time, and examine the contents of all the pans on the fire, and ascertain whether they contained any part of the stolen property. In the same locality the paid constables were directed to tap with their staves the pockets of all labourers or other persons found out after dark, in order that any pheasant's or partridge's eggs therein might be broken.
>
> In conformity with the directions of the chief magistrate of one considerable town, the constable seized all vagrants found within his jurisdiction and took them to prison, where their heads were shaved, and they were then set at liberty.

The original powers of constables were seen to have been exercised in a variety of original ways:

> The superintendent of the new police of one town was asked – You are sometimes obliged to pursue without warrants, are you not? – I never wait for warrants – it is not my plan. It is a waste of time. The magistrate's clerk was rather particular about it, because, I believe, every warrant was something to him. I said they are things I do not know much about. I rarely act upon a thing that is not very clear. I am for being prompt in everything. I act first and take the responsibility afterwards. I say if I can take the man up with a warrant, I can take him up without a warrant.[3]

The commissioners recommended that there should be a combined national force directly responsible to Parliament and through Parliament to the public. Such a force would act 'in subordination to

[1] They were Charles Shaw Lefevre, Charles Rowan and Edwin Chadwick. Chadwick's views on police are described in Radzinowicz, *History of English Criminal Law*, Vol. 3, Chap. 14. He was engaged by Jeremy Bentham to write a section on police for Bentham's Constitutional Code.

[2] See especially *First Report of the Constabulary Force Commissioners, 1839*.

[3] *Ibid.*, pp. 327, 328.

general directions from one general and responsible executive authority'.[1] In the event Chadwick's solution was not adopted and except in the metropolis the clear-cut answerability which accompanied it has been implicitly rejected. In its place there has developed an ambiguous set of local relationships sometimes tolerated or even welcomed as if it were the only alternative to a Ministry of Justice and a national police.

The growth of a thesis of police independence has also no doubt been assisted by the fear of partisan political interference with police duties by local authorities dominated by political or commercial interests. Certainly in the middle years of the nineteenth century administration by watch committees was often squalid. The Select Committee on Police which reported to Parliament in the 1850s drew attention to the influence of brewers in a number of boroughs.

At Norwich 'the influence of the brewers on the watch committee was such that the chief constable was under instructions not to prosecute any publican without the approval of the committee. When he defied the rule he was dismissed.'[2] Professional police forces were, of course, a recently accepted phenomenon of English government. In an essay on 'The Constabulary' in his *Justice and Police* published in 1885, Maitland was able to say of the statutory organization of police. 'All this is very new; it has come into existence during the last sixty years; indeed down to 1856 there was no law for the whole of England requiring that there should be paid policemen. The general law was that each township should have its constable.' The word 'police' he adds, 'did not, I think, become common until late in the last century. Johnson just admits it, but only as a French word used in England . . . The group of words, police, policy, polity, politics, politic, political, politician is a good example of delicate distinctions.'[3] In outlining the status of constables, Maitland mentions

[1] *Ibid.*, pp. 331, 349.
[2] Henry Parris, 'The Home Office and the Provincial Police in England and Wales, 1856–1870', *1961 Public Law*, p. 251.
[3] *Justice and Police*, p. 105. Radzinowicz (*op. cit.*, Vol. 3, p. 1) says that the word in its modern sense was almost unknown in the early part of the eighteenth century and when introduced was 'regarded with the utmost suspicion as a portent of the sinister power which held France in its grip'.

27

the common law duty of arresting offenders and the general duty of obeying the lawful orders of the justices. There is no mention or suggestion anywhere in Maitland's essay of any constabulary immunity from control as to the policy to be pursued in the exercise of common law powers.

The compatibility of common law constabulary powers with administrative direction by police authorities and justices seems to have been assumed by all the statutory provisions for police forces in the nineteenth century. That fact is clearest in the case of the metropolitan provisions where the police authority was the Secretary of State for Home Affairs directly in control of the force and answerable for it to Parliament. The preamble of the Metropolitan Police Act of 1829 recited that there was to be set up a new Office of Police acting under the immediate authority of the Secretary of State which should direct and control the whole of this new system of police. Yet the constables who were to be directed and controlled were to have 'all such powers, authorities, privileges and advantages and to be liable to all such duties and responsibilities as any constable duly appointed now has or hereafter may have within his constablewick'. In other words the new police were to exercise by statute all the powers of common law constables and there was no recognition that either the control of the Secretary of State or the lawful orders of the justices which they were enjoined to obey were in any way incompatible with the exercise of the common law powers which were preserved. The notion of lawful directions is similarly written into the statutes relating to county and borough forces. The County Police Act of 1839 refers to a chief constable's being subject to 'such lawful orders as he may receive from the justices in general or quarter sessions'; and the County and Borough Police Act of 1856 provides that constables acting under the Municipal Corporations Act, 1835, and the County Police Acts of 1839 and 1840 shall 'perform all such duties . . . as the justices in general or quarter sessions assembled, or the Watch Committees of such respective counties and boroughs from time to time direct and require'. The Municipal Corporations Act, 1882, provided that constables should be liable to all such duties and responsibilities as any constable had – at common law or by statute (s. 191, subs. 2). Similarly, the Police (Scotland) Act of 1857 and its successors (consolidated in 1956) both gave the police the common law powers of constables and subjected them to the lawful orders of burgh magistrates and sheriffs. The appropriate chief constable was to comply with such instructions whether general or as respects any particular case, 'in directing the constables of a police force in the performance of their duty'.[1]

The similarity in fact of the provision in the Metropolitan, Scottish, and English County and Borough legislation for directions from justices suggests that in each case an important traditional form of subordination and supervision was preserved.

THE METROPOLITAN POSITION

One might indeed wonder whether there is any reason at all for believing that chief constables in the provinces have ever been visited by any peculiar autonomy of status going beyond the moral right to that respect for the decisions of an executive officer which is recognized as desirable even where, as in the metropolitan area, the constitutional position is clearly one that rules out anything in the nature of autonomy in policy matters.[2] The metropolitan position, in fact, points to an incongruity in the conclusions of *Fisher v. Oldham Corporation*, and the sort of deduction normally made from them in the books. Constables are constables in Hammersmith as in Oldham. The status of the Metropolitan Police Commissioner, moreover, raises some doubt as to whether any conclusions about independence of direction necessarily follow from the holding of any particular kind of office under the Crown. The Commissioner is appointed 'for preservation of the peace, the prevention of crimes [and] the detection and committal of offenders'. He is an officer appointed by Royal Warrant, but he is undisputably subject on some matters to direction by the Home Secretary.

Nobody seems to have complained, in the twentieth century at

---

[1] Police (Scotland) Act, 1956, s. 4.
[2] 'The Metropolitan Police are the direct responsibility of the Home Secretary. It is his responsibility. He can give orders to the Metropolitan Police and they are bound to obey them.' (314 H.C. Deb. 5s. col. 1554.)

any rate, about a danger to constitutional principles in the sub-ordination of metropolitan constables, chief officers, and the Com-missioner, to policy control of their functions (outside the auto-matic application of the processes of criminal justice). Members of the House of Commons have complained, in fact, in the opposite sense of the iniquity of a situation in which the constituents of Members for metropolitan constituencies could write to their Member about the conduct or misconduct of the police whilst con-stituents of Members sitting for provincial constituencies could not, because of the responsibilities of watch committees.[1] The parlia-mentary implication of this situation must surely have been that in some degree local elected authorities stood in a similar relation to the police as the House of Commons did for the metropolis. Although there have been suggestions by Ministers (and on occasion by the Speaker)[2] that Members pursued matters of too trivial a nature, there is no question but that for the metropolitan police the Secre-tary of State accepts an extremely wide and detailed responsibility.[3] Sir William Joynson-Hicks in 1928 in the course of a debate on the Savidge case spoke of the 'democratic control' of the House over the police and described the metropolitan force as 'an Imperial force directed by the Secretary of State on behalf of the Commons'. 'I am,' he added, 'the servant of the House of Commons and every action I take, every decision I come to in regard to the police, can be brought up and discussed here.'[4] Clearly answerability to the Commons is not thought, in the metropolis, to be irreconcilable with 'answerability to the law' and the performance of the common law duties of a constable.

In 1957 Mr J. E. S. Simon, Joint Under-Secretary of State, spoke of the relations between the Metropolitan Police Commissioner and the Home Secretary in the following terms. It was, he said, 'the Secretary of State's sphere to prescribe and enforce general prin-

[1] E.g. 585 H.C. Deb. 5s. col. 570-1. See also Chap. 4 below.

[2] 210 Parl. Deb. 3s. col. 596 (1872).

[3] Even for such details as the purchase of bicycles for the Metropolitan force (575 H.C. Deb. 5s. col. 87) or the type of summer clothing worn by policemen (572 H.C. Deb. 5s. col. 1292).

[4] 220 H.C. Deb. 5s. cols. 839-40.

30

ciples, and the Commissioner's sphere to apply them to individual cases, subject only to his general accountability to the Secretary of State as Police Authority'.[1] In the nineteenth century the subordination of the Commissioner was perhaps less clear. More than one Commissioner claimed a degree of constitutional autonomy, but the position was emphatically restated in the House in 1888 after disagreement between the Home Secretary and his Commissioner Sir Charles Warren had led to the latter's resignation, the question in issue being the methods used in suppressing public disorder in London. Sir William Harcourt stated the position in the following terms. It would, he said, be an unwise Secretary of State who unduly interfered with the executive authority of the Commissioner. They should act together as confidential colleagues. But he had never before heard the question raised as to how far the Secretary of State had the right to direct the Commissioner or how far the Commissioner was bound to conform to his wishes. For a Commissioner to declare a condition of independence he never could have conceived possible. Such a state of affairs, he added, would be intolerable. It would result in an authority responsible to no government or municipality in control of an army of 14,000 men, at whose mercy the civil community would be. One might discuss whether such a force should be under a municipal or a governmental authority, but the notion of its being independent of either was a doctrine so unconstitutional as to appear absurd. What, he asked, would Sir Robert Peel have thought of it? It was, he concluded, a matter entirely at the discretion of the Secretary of State how far the principle of responsible authority should interfere with executive action. The Commissioner knew his force and the way its work might best be accomplished, and the less interference the better. But 'for the policy of the police . . . the Secretary of State must be and is solely responsible'. Such a question as to whether a public meeting was to be prohibited was 'not a question of police but a question of policy'.[2]

Sir William Harcourt's propositions do not in their general aspect

[1] 571 H.C. Deb. 5s. col. 574. See also Chap. 4 below.
[2] 330 Parl. Deb. 3s. col. 1163.

appear to be unduly dependent upon the metropolitan character of the police force in question. This conclusion was in fact drawn in the 1888 debate by the Home Secretary, Mr Henry Matthews. What Harcourt had laid down ought, he said, to hold good in the large provincial towns. It would be intolerable if 'in any large town the commander of the police force or of any other force should hold irresponsible authority'. That was a position 'which could not be allowed to be assumed by the chief constable of any of the large towns of the country'.[1] His view, like that of Sir William Harcourt, was that in the case of the metropolitan force it had been the intention of the legislature to establish ministerial responsibility 'not for every detail of the management of the force, but in regard to the general policy of the police in the discharge of their duty'.[2]

There seems no overwhelming reason for believing that the general principles laid down by Harcourt and Matthews in relation to both metropolitan and local forces have ceased to apply. Nothing which has occurred since 1888 obviously overthrows the inference that the relations between any police authority and its chief constable should be in principle similar to those governing the relations between the Home Secretary and the Metropolitan Police Commissioner. The Commissioner's relationship to the Home Secretary helps to demonstrate that a constitutionally subordinate position with respect to policy is compatible both with the concession of a measure of practical independence in such matters as police discipline, and with non-interference in matters involving the routine processes of justice and prosecution.

[1] 330 Parl. Deb. 3s. col. 1174.
[2] *Ibid.*, col. 1174. Sir Frank Newsam in *The Home Office* (1954), p. 45, quotes this remark with approval, as did Sir Edward Troup in the old Whitehall series (*The Home Office*, (1925), p. 104).

3 Fisher v. Oldham and the Independence of Constables

YET IN THE TWENTIETH CENTURY THERE HAS BEEN CON-trived out of the common law position a novel and surprising thesis, which is sometimes now to be heard intoned as if it were a thing of antiquity with its roots alongside Magna Carta. It is succinctly put in a sentence used by Sir John Anderson in an article on Police written in 1929. 'The policeman is nobody's servant . . . he executes a public office under the Law and it is the Law . . . which is the policeman's master.'[1] From this proposition a wider thesis has been inferred to the effect that:

> The police authority have no right to give the chief constable orders about the disposition of the force or the way in which police duty should be carried out, and he cannot divest himself of responsibility by turning to them for guidance or instructions on matters of police duty.[2]

This view has often been repeated and elaborated. In 1958 Lord Chesham, speaking on behalf of the Government, said:

> No police authority or anyone else has any authority to interfere in relation to the enforcement of the law by the police . . . the full responsi-bility for enforcement is a matter which is reserved entirely to the chief officer of police. In the exercise of this responsibility he is answerable to the law alone and not to any police authority.[3]

A collection of sentiments equally emphatic could easily be as-sembled. In sum they may appear to represent a solid and impressive

[1] 'The Police' (*Public Administration*, 1929, p. 192).
[2] Cmd. 7831 para. 185 (Report of the Oaksey Committee on Police Conditions of Service).
[3] 213 H.L. Deb. 5s. col. 47.

body of testimony and are often cited as such. Yet the majority of these opinions are merely self-reinforcing and stand upon a kind of inverted pyramid. The legal apex of the pyramid is the opinion of Mr Justice McCardie in *Fisher v. Oldham Corporation* decided in 1930. Support for the edifice has been supplied by a certain number of other decisions both before and after the *Fisher* case in which various issues of civil liability were raised affecting police constables.

The constitutional doctrine of the immunity of constables from orders or instructions in their office of keeping the peace does not, it should be noticed, rest upon any direct judicial statement in an inquiry directed to that precise question. It is conceivable that it might have been so established as a proposition of English public law – as for example by an action for a declaration on an occasion when an attempt had been made to give purportedly valid instructions to the police. But no such case has been reported. The modern thesis rests almost entirely upon fairly recent inferences from the law of civil liability. In particular it derives from the doctrine that there is no master and servant relationship between constables and their employers in the rather special sense which has been given to that phrase in the law of torts. Two sorts of situation have given rise to the decisions. In one of these the police authority (or, in other jurisdictions, the Crown as employer) has been the defendant in an action for damages for the wrongful act of a constable. In the other type of case the employing police authority has sued a third party for loss of services resulting from an injury to its employee. Tactical considerations have dictated variations in the arguments advanced from one case to another. In the first type of case in which a police authority is sued, its interest has been to plead that no master-servant relationship exists and that the authority is not vicariously liable for the torts of its appointee. In the second type of case where the police authority or the Crown has been the aggrieved party, its interest has been to claim that the master-servant relationship does exist and that its 'servant' has been injured. That either argument has been advanced according to circumstance may be explained in terms of a prudent regard for the taxpayers' money, or alternatively as displaying a proper awareness that the concept of 'service' may assume different meanings in different contexts. There seems, however, to have been no reluctance to assume on the basis of these cases that the *constitutional* relationship between police and police authorities may be directly inferred from the law of master and 'servant'.

FISHER V. OLDHAM CORPORATION

In the *Fisher* case[1] it was sought to make the corporation of the borough of Oldham liable in damages for the actions of the Oldham police. Curiously, this seems to have been the first occasion in England (though not in Scotland) when such an action had been brought. The facts briefly were as follows. Fisher, a Plaistow timber merchant, was arrested in London and taken to Oldham to be charged with obtaining money by false pretences. After having been detained for several hours he was found not to be the man for whose arrest a warrant had been issued. He was released and sued the corporation. His statement of claim alleged that 'the defendants acting through their watch committee are the police authority for the County Borough of Oldham and are the employers of the police for the said borough'. McCardie J., in a much-quoted judgment, first of all rehearsed the relevant provisions of the Municipal Corporations Act of 1882. By that Act it had been provided that watch committees might frame such regulations as they should deem expedient for preventing neglect or abuse and for making borough constables efficient in the discharge of their duties. They might at any time suspend or dismiss a constable whom they thought negligent or unfit.[2] On the basis of this it was contended that the defendants, having a duty to pay salary or wages, a power to make regulations and a power to dismiss, were placed by the statute substantially in a master and servant relationship.

However, other statutory provisions (McCardie J. continued) had given to the Home Secretary, as central police authority, a power to make regulations as to the government, mutual aid, pay, allowances, pensions, clothing, expenses and conditions of service.[3] In addition

[1] [1930] 2 K.B. 364.
[2] Municipal Corporations Act, 1882, s. 191 subs. 3 and 4.
[3] Police Act, 1919, s. 4.

the Police Appeals Act, 1927, had provided that the Secretary of State should hear appeals from dismissals by watch committees. Taking these together with the common law view of the status of police officers it became clear that the police in effecting the arrest and detention of the plaintiff were fulfilling their duties as public servants and officers of the crown and the corporation were not answerable in law for their actions. Judgment was given for the defendants.

Much weight has been placed on this decision. How exactly did McCardie J. arrive at the conclusion that constables, despite their local connections, were 'servants of the state' and 'officers of the Crown or central power'? There is first of all the matter of the Home Secretary's powers. But these were primarily powers to standardize the conditions of service and to secure uniformity in material conditions. They hardly seem in themselves sufficient to support a conclusion that the police are an emanation of central government. That inference rests essentially upon the passages in the judgment which deal with the status of constables at common law and with a handful of earlier decisions in which police functions had figured directly or indirectly.

In addition there are certain passages in which the suggested consequences of holding police to be servants of the watch committee are sketched out. 'Suppose [it was said] that a police officer arrested a man for a serious felony. Suppose, too, that the watch committee of the borough at once passed a resolution directing that the felon should be released. Of what value would such a resolution be? Not only would it be the plain duty of the police officer to disregard the resolution, but it would also be the duty of the chief constable to consider whether an information should not at once be laid against the members of the watch committee for a conspiracy to obstruct the course of criminal justice.'[1] The consequence suggested is that 'If the local authorities are to be liable in such a case as this for the acts of the police with respect to felons and misdemeanours, then it would indeed be a serious matter and it would entitle them to demand that they ought to secure a full measure of control over the arrest and prosecution of all offenders.'[2]

[1] [1930] 2 K.B. 364 at 372–3.   [2] *Ibid.*

It might, however, be thought that the particular example chosen here is insufficient to support so general a conclusion. A watch committee resolution which is an instigation to interfere with the process of criminal justice would be plainly an illegal order and it would be the duty of the police to disregard it for that reason independently of any special relationship between police and watch committee.

THE CROWN CONNECTION ARGUMENT

Considerable emphasis was placed by McCardie J. on an observation of Lord Blackburn in *Coomber v. Berkshire Justices* that 'the administration of justice ... and the preservation of order and prevention of crime by means of what is now called police are among the most important functions of Government [and] by the constitution of this country these functions do of common right belong to the Crown'.[1] 'The whole *ratio decidendi* of *Coomber's* case', he added, 'was that the police were the servants of the Crown.' But it is open to question whether *Coomber's* case can really be relied upon as establishing that proposition in any general sense. What was in issue on that occasion was whether a block of buildings used for various local government purposes, but partly used for police and judicial purposes, was exempt from taxation. It had been unclear whether the exemption of property used for Crown and governmental purposes extended to such premises. Lord Bramwell stated his opinion in terms wider than those implied by McCardie J., saying explicitly that the *ratio decidendi* of the case was that the purposes of the police were 'public' purposes or purposes 'required for the government of the country'. The other two opinions were those of Lords Blackburn and Watson. Blackburn suggested that the police were in *consimili casu* to Crown servants. Watson thought that they were not Crown servants, distinguishing between police and servants of the Crown such as Post Office and Admiralty officials, the former not being in his view strictly speaking Crown servants.

McCardie's judgment refers to the approval of *Coomber's* case by the Privy Council in 1927 in *Metropolitan Meat Industry Board v. Sheedy*.[2] Here again, however, the question in issue was whether a

---

[1] (1883) 9 App. Cas. 61, 71.   [2] [1927] A.C. 899, 903.

board administering the meat industry in New South Wales could be held to share the financial immunity of the Crown. It was said that the shield of the Crown had been extended (in earlier decisions on exemption from rates and taxes) to services which might be described as part of 'the public government of the country'. Since *Fisher's* case was decided similar decisions have had to be made by the courts in relation to a number of public bodies and nationalized services. The Transport Commission (as it was in 1950) was held to have none of the Crown's immunities.[1] A different conclusion has been reached about Regional Hospital Boards.[2] But no one would think of drawing general inferences about Hospital Board employees similar to those drawn in *Fisher's* case about police constables simply on the ground that for a particular purpose the service in which they are employed shares a privilege enjoyed by the Crown and its servants. This is all that the Crown connection in *Coomber v. Berkshire Justices* so heavily accented in *Fisher's* case really amounts to. Since 1930 it has become clear that in more important constitutional contexts the police are not to be regarded as Crown servants at all. The Crown Proceedings Act of 1947 refers for example to 'officers', 'agents' and 'servants' of the Crown. Whatever the difference between these may be, the police are none of them for purposes of the Act. Its criteria are that officers of the Crown, for the purpose of Crown Proceedings, must be directly or indirectly appointed by the Crown and paid wholly out of the consolidated fund or money otherwise voted by Parliament.[3] In neither respect do the police qualify. The police undoubtedly owe allegiance to the Crown, but this characteristic they share with British subjects in general. For purposes of the Official Secrets Acts a police constable has been held also to be a 'person holding office under His Majesty'. But that is not sufficient to make him an officer or servant of the Crown. Lord Hewart's remarks in the case in question make the point effectively. The justices, he said, had 'apparently been under the impression that a person who serves His Majesty must necessarily

[1] *Tamlin v. Hannaford* [1950] K.B. 18.
[2] *Nottingham No. 1 Area Hospital Management Committee v. Owen* [1958] 1 Q.B. 50.
[3] Crown Proceedings Act. S 2(6).

hold office under His Majesty. That, however, is not the case. There are many offices which are held under His Majesty the holders of which are not in any proper sense in the service of His Majesty.'[1]

The ordinary facts about the employment of police officers might also have been used to throw doubt upon McCardie's view that the police were for constitutional purposes officers of the Crown rather than of local authorities. The Crown does not appoint policemen. It does not dismiss them and it does not equip them. It is a very odd servant whose master does none of these things. A police constable might reasonably have been thought (for purposes other than civil liability) to be in the service of those who did.

THE 'MASTER AND SERVANT' ARGUMENT

Nevertheless the language of civil liability has undoubtedly influenced, and even determined, that used to describe the constitutional relationship between police and police authorities. It is interesting to see how this came to be so. The connection between the two sorts of question, as it appeared in 1930, lay in the fact that vicarious liability of the employer in tort had historically turned upon the degree of control which employers were able to exercise over their servants in relation to any particular activity alleged to be wrongful.

It is remarkable that when the action was brought by Fisher against Oldham Corporation in 1930, counsel were unable to cite any English decision in which the civil liability of a police authority for the activities of its constables had been determined. Unsuccessful attempts were, however, made in Scotland during the nineteenth century to fix responsibility on various local bodies. Two may be noted:

Leask v. County Council of Stirling.[2] In this case, reported in 1893, the pursuer, a sailor who had been wrongfully arrested, sued the county council as employer. It was held that he was not their servant

---

[1] *Lewis v. Cattle* [1938] 2 K.B. 454, 457.
[2] 1 S.L.T. (1893) 241. Cf. *Girdwood v. Standing Joint Committee of the County of Midlothian* (1845) 22 R. 11, and *Muir v. Burgh of Hamilton* 1 S.L.T. 164 (1910).

but that of the standing joint committee to whom the management of the police had been entrusted. Lack of success here followed from picking the wrong employer rather than failure to establish a relation of employment in general.

Adamson v. Martin.[1] Here the action was brought against a chief constable by a boy of seventeen after the taking of his fingerprints and photographs by a detective. It was held irrelevant for lack of any averment that the detective was acting on the instructions of the chief constable. The failure to establish vicarious liability in a case such as this did not entail any argument that the detectives were not subject to instructions from their chief constable or under his control.

In none of the Scottish cases, however, where actions were brought against local authorities did anyone succeed in making the appointing body liable.[2]

In England, on the other hand, no one seems even to have tried. An implicit assumption can be found that an analogy existed between the police and certain other officials for whose actions local authorities had been held in certain circumstances not to be liable. It was to this analogy that McCardie J. had perforce in 1930 to turn. He was able to cite a passage from a case decided just after the turn of the century in which Wills J. had remarked that 'Nobody has ever heard of a corporation being made liable for the negligence of a police officer in the performance of his duties'. The facts of this case are of some importance in tracing the origins of the doctrine which found its way into *Fisher's* case.

Stanbury v. Exeter Corporation.[3] Though police functions were brought into the argument they were not here directly involved. The issue related to certain statutory functions performed by an inspector appointed by a local authority under the Diseases of Animals Act of 1894. The inspector was alleged to have been negli-

---

[1] 1916 S.C. 319.
[2] For the cases see *Encyclopedia of the Laws of Scotland*, Vol. 11, pp. 376–416.
[3] [1905] 2 K.B. 838.

gent in seizing and detaining sheep and the authority were sued. The inspector's duties in the matter in question were set out, however, with some precision in a regulation made under the Act of Parliament (the Sheep Scab order, 1898). The regulation instructed him that on receiving in any manner whatsoever information of the supposed existence of the disease or having reasonable ground to suspect it, he should 'proceed with all practicable speed to the place where such disease . . . exists and . . . there and elsewhere put in force and discharge the powers and duties conferred and imposed on him as inspector by or under the Act of 1894 and this order'.

In these circumstances the inspector was held by the court to be 'controlled by the superior and paramount authority of the Board of Agriculture'. The authority who appointed him were not liable since in this instance his statutory duty was to carry out not their instructions but, in effect, those of the Board of Agriculture. The absence of master and servant liability was not, it may be seen, founded upon any general immunity or discretionary power but upon the existence of a duty to carry out these mandatory instructions. Counsel for the defendants, however, had suggested in the course of their argument that the inspector fell into a class of officials for whose negligent acts local authorities were not liable. His position, it was urged, was analogous to that of a police officer. Upon this point it was conceded that there was no English authority but certain American decisions mentioned in Beven on *Negligence* were cited; Wills J. appears to have approved the principle adumbrated in these cases to the effect that the duties of the police were of a public or national kind and had no purely local characteristics.

This transatlantic principle noted by Beven and accepted in *Stanbury v. Exeter Corporation* thus seems to be the judicial starting point, in England at any rate, of the twentieth-century view of the constable's immunities. Interestingly enough, Beven himself expressed some doubt about the logic of the American decisions as applied to English circumstances. In the third edition of his textbook[1] the author was able to incorporate the decision in the Exeter case

[1] *Negligence in Law* (3rd ed., 1908), pp. 327–8.

decided three years earlier and his comments are of some interest. The test which Wills J. had accepted, he thought, reflected the stress laid in the United States on the distinction between duties exercised by 'the State as a part of its sovereignty', and private or corporate powers. No such principle, he suggested, had hitherto been accepted in England. He continued: 'The test in America may be all right; in England it is merely an evasion of the issue which is surely whether the officers (whatever the duties they perform) are made accountable to the local authority.'

At this stage, therefore, we see an uncertainly based rule which, by an analogy whose force is not beyond doubt, places the police in a class of officials whose employers might in certain circumstances for various reasons escape vicarious liability. In a case reported in the year following the Exeter decision the analogy was reinforced by litigation arising in Tasmania which directly involved police functions.

Enever v. The King.[1] In an action under the Tasmanian Crown Redress Act the High Court of Australia accepted the rule enunciated in *Stanbury v. Exeter Corporation* as being applicable to police constables. Griffith C.J. however had some doubts about the principle involved and propounded 'a sounder basis for the rule of immunity for those who appoint constables . . . than that suggested by Wills J.' (i.e. than that founded on the distinction between 'local' and 'national, public or state' functions). A constable's powers, the Chief Justice suggested, were conferred by law and were 'definite and limited'. Therefore there could be 'no suggestion of holding him out as a person possessed of greater authority than the law confers upon him'. The conclusion was that a constable 'when acting as a peace officer is not exercising a delegated authority but an original authority and the general law of agency has no application'.[2]

In both *Stanbury v. Exeter* and *Enever v. The King*, one very clear strand of argument appears, namely that the employers were not liable because the duties of the persons appointed were in the relevant

---

[1] (1906) 3 C.L.R. 969.   [2] At p. 977.

respects 'fixed and defined'. In the first case this was so because of the provisions of a particular statute and the regulations made under it: in the second case it was assumed to follow from the powers of arrest conferred on constables[1] (the case involved an allegation of wrongful arrest). On the assumption that there was no detailed control over the manner in which the particular disputed duties were carried out it was understandable at that time[2] that no master and servant relationship should have been held to exist. Unfortunately, however, the assumption about the 'definite and limited' powers of the police was made fairly summarily, since attention was focused upon powers of arrest. The assumption cannot be carried over without argument to all police operations and enforcement measures. The degree of general control by police authorities which existed in these fields or was constitutionally proper was never discussed in any detail in these vicarious liability cases at the turn of the century. It was not necessary to do so. Yet once it had been held that no relationship of master and servant existed for purposes of civil liability it became possible to expand the particular finding about lack of control into a general assumption of independence in all

[1] A similar conclusion was reached in *British South Africa Co. v. Crickmore*, 1921 App. D. 107, where a constable employed by the company was held *in exercising powers of arrest* to be acting not on the company's behalf but in obedience to the commands of legislation.

The South African courts, however, have confined the principle to the duty of arrest and in general have found no difficulty in admitting constables to be servants employed by the Crown. In *Sibaya v. Swart*, 1950 (4) S.A.L.R. 515 (A.D.), for example, the Crown were held liable when a constable assaulted the appellant after arresting him. Centlivres J.A. said 'A policeman is engaged by the Crown to perform not only the duties entrusted to him by his superior officers but also the duties he has to perform in terms of the statutory law and it seems to me that in both cases he is under the control and subject to the commands of his employer, namely the Crown'. Only a statutory duty of a personal nature, such as an arrest itself, appears to stand outside the master servant relation as defined in these cases.

[2] It may be noted that the existence of a master servant relationship for purposes of establishing vicarious liability is no longer universally thought to rest upon the existence of detailed control over the function performed. Various other considerations have been advanced. In *Cassidy v. Minister of Health*, for example, the view of Denning L.J. was that 'The reason why the employers are liable in such cases is not because they can control the way in which the work is done . . . but because they . . . have chosen them for the task and have in their hands the ultimate sanction for good behaviour, the power of dismissal.' [1951] 2 K.B. 343. Cf. J. C. Fleming, *Law of Torts*, Chap. 17.

matters pertaining to law enforcement and keeping of the peace. Clearly this wider inference lacked justification.

Attorney-General for New South Wales v. Perpetual Trustee Company.[1] In the 1950s another Australian decision was considered indirectly to have endorsed the doctrine in *Fisher's* case. On this occasion an employing authority (here the Crown) was trying to establish rather than to deny the existence of a service relationship. A police constable in the New South Wales police force had been injured in a collision between a motor vehicle and the tramcar in which he was travelling. The Crown claimed various sums in respect of his disablement in an action *per quod servitium amisit.*

The High Court of Australia and the Privy Council shared the view that for the purpose in question police constables were not servants and that the Crown could not recover for loss of their services. The decision has been taken, therefore, as indicating further judicial support for the implications drawn from *Fisher's* case. As with *Fisher's* case, however, it may be argued that the decision has no direct bearing on the more general question of *constitutional* independence. Though the exact scope of the action for loss of services may be difficult to assess,[2] it would be substantially true to say that the New South Wales case decided that the domestic relation of master and servant upon which the old common law action had turned was not to be extended to modern public 'services'. The Privy Council did not dissent from the view expressed in the High Court of Australia that for the purposes of this particular action the service relationship of a constable was not in principle distinguishable from that of a soldier. It was a mistake to suppose (Viscount Simonds suggested) that the action for loss of services would lie simply because there was in some sense a contract of service or because a man is a servant of the Crown.[3] The mutability of the concept of 'service' and 'servant' from context to context is

[1] (1952) 85 C.L.R. 237 and [1955] A.C. 457.

[2] Cf. *Commissioner for Railways v. Scott* (1959) Austr. Law Journal Reports 126. See also G. Jones, 'Per Quod Servitium Amisit' 74 *Law Quarterly Review* 39: A. G. Guest, 34 *Canadian Bar Review* 1078, and 38 *Canadian Bar Review* 104.

[3] [1955] A.C. 457 at 477 ff.

evident. It is equally evident from a consideration of the decision in *Inland Revenue Commissioners v. Hambrook*[1] in which the Court of Appeal later held that in the same context civil servants also were not 'servants'.

One may conclude that the New South Wales case, though often quoted in works on police, is of no more relevance to them in the constitutional context than it is to the constitutional position of soldiers or civil servants. No one would think of inferring in the latter cases any general autonomy of action from the absence of a 'service' relationship of the kind in question in the New South Wales case. Indeed it was part of the successful argument against the Crown in that case that persons who were not 'servants' in the sense under dispute could be subject to the strictest discipline and orders. Military and civil employees of the Crown obviously provide an example. There is admittedly one form of constitutional independence exercised by the armed forces. They must deploy independent judgment in exercising a right to disobey manifestly illegal commands. So must constables. But the independence involved in a right to reject illegal orders does not entail independence in the sense of an immunity from subjection to lawful orders. It would be fair to conclude that no such immunity and no general constitutional autonomy can be inferred from the much-handled civil liability cases, including *Fisher v. Oldham*.

[1] [1956] 2 Q.B. 641.

4 Local and Parliamentary Responsibility Before the 1964 Act

THE THEORY OF CONSTABULARY INDEPENDENCE HAS HAD A considerable impact on legislative accountability for police work. Despite the theory, as we have seen, the Home Secretary as police authority for the metropolitan area has been open to parliamentary question on a wide range of metropolitan police matters. It might well have been supposed that questions in local council chambers by local representatives addressed to the chairmen of watch committees as local police authorities would have been the accepted form of legislative responsibility outside the metropolitan area. But this has not been so. Local accountability has been hindered and its operation rendered uncertain both by the supposed legal status of constables and by the existence of the Home Secretary's statutory powers. In Parliament distinctions have been drawn between the Home Secretary's concern for police efficiency and his lack of responsibility for police operations. Ministers and the Speaker have sometimes, in commenting on the latter point, implied that a parallel form of local accountability for the police in fact existed. Mr Speaker Lowther, for example, in 1917 ruled a Member's question about the handling of a local riot to be out of order with the words: 'The hon. Member should ask the watch committee of the district. The great boast of England is its system of local government.'[1] More recently a ruling in 1958, holding a Private Member's motion on the powers of chief constables to be inadmissible, stated that:

Day to day administration of a county police force or other local authority police force . . . lies in the hands of the local councillors who

[1] 93 H.C. Deb. 5s. col. 1613.

are elected persons and ultimately in the hands of local government electors.[1]

Members have sometimes been told in categorical terms that the Secretary of State could give no orders to local police and hence was not accountable for their activities since they were under the control of watch committees and standing joint committees. Being made for the purpose of emphasizing in the strongest possible way the lack of central responsibility such statements have incautiously presented a thoroughly misleading picture of the local position. In fact the right of local representatives to put questions on, or to secure debate of, police matters has been by no means clear. There has been a double obstacle. Not only has there been doubt about the degree of control which could be exercised by the police authority over its police, but also a lack of direct responsibility of the statutory police authority to the local authority itself, since the decisions of a watch committee in non-financial matters have not in law required the approval of the parent council.[2] In the face of these uncertainties different practices have been adopted in different localities. In the evidence presented to the Royal Commission it was stated that, as a matter of practice, debates took place in some borough councils on the actions of the police and of the watch committee but that council members had in law no right to raise such matters. County councillors were in a similar position. The point was made fairly bluntly in the House of Commons in December 1963 by a Member serving (as a magistrate) on a county standing joint committee. 'No member of a standing joint committee,' he said, 'is answerable to anybody. Once I have been elected by the Quarter Sessions of Denbighshire to represent them on the standing joint committee I can do as I like and I am answerable to no one. The same is true of the county councillors. No member of a county council at a meeting can challenge a county councillor about any action of his as a member of the standing joint committee.'[3] Until 1964 what happened in practice in each authority

[1] 586 H.C. Deb. 5s. col. 1295.
[2] Presumably a council could, if dissatisfied, dismiss its watch committee and appoint another, but this is hardly a practicable way of securing normal accountability.
[3] Police Bill, Standing Committee D, cols. 42–3.

largely depended upon the view of the Town Clerk, and on the views of the watch committee's chairman. A member of the public, wishing to raise some matter of police administration or to criticize the activities of the police, has been, equally with his elected member, without any clear-cut recourse. He might address himself to the Town Clerk, who might agree to place the matter on the watch committee agenda if he thought it proper for the watch committee's consideration. But there has been no guarantee that the committee or the Clerk would inform the complainant of any conclusions reached or action taken.

Both local councillors and Members of Parliament have experienced the frustration which this ambivalent situation produced. It was exemplified on a number of occasions in the 1930s when Fascist disturbances occurred in London and the provinces. The provincial disturbances both underlined the uncertainty about central responsibility for police matters and led to exaggeration in the House of Commons of the extent to which local police authorities exercised or acknowledged the duty to control police operations. One such episode, which illustrates the difficulty, originated in a meeting addressed by Sir Oswald Mosley in Oxford on 25 May 1936, which ended in disorder and was followed by complaints that the police were insufficiently active in preventing breaches of the peace. An eye-witness account printed in the *Oxford Mail* ran as follows:

Mr M. U. S. Hunter of Christ Church said he observed a column of Blackshirt stewards moving slowly up the centre gangway in a menacing manner . . . 'I went to the end of the Hall where the Chief Constable and the Superintendent of Police were standing and asked the chief constable whether according to the Lord Chancellor's regulations it was legal to block up the gangway with this crowd of stewards.

'Mr Fox told me to mind my own business and on my repeating my question told me to run away.

'Eventually Mosley gave the signal to throw one man out. The twenty-odd stewards leaped on the man in a body, severely mauling him; the rest of the audience rose to the defence and the fight started. All this was easily foreseeable and since it is the duty of the police to prevent

48

breaches of the peace before they happen I cannot understand their non-interference.'[1]

In the course of the mêlée the present Lord Longford (then the Hon. Frank Pakenham) was roughly handled, according to the same report, 'in attempting to rescue a diminutive undergraduate from the stewards'. His subsequent attempt to enlist the aid of the police was described by him in a letter to *The Times*:

> . . . I made a statement to the police soon after the meeting saying that, when called upon I could supply the names of witnesses who could probably identify my assailants. But the chief constable never asked me for the names in question; never, I understand, approached the doctor referred to in my statement for medical evidence and announced a week after my statement had been made that no steps had been taken to trace those who assaulted me 'as the complainant has not said that he can identify his alleged assailants.'
>
> These are some of the difficulties that confront a victim of Fascist violence who himself struck no blow in his attempt at rescue work.[2]

The Oxford meeting was the subject of a Parliamentary question to the Home Secretary by Mr Hugh Dalton who asked Sir John Simon whether he was aware that the Hon. Frank Pakenham, a fellow and tutor of Christ Church, had been violently assaulted and injured at a public meeting and had received no assistance either at

[1] *Oxford Mail*, 26 May 1936.

[2] *The Times*, 11 July 1936. The account given in Lord Longford's autobiography (*Born to Believe*, p. 83) suggests that the final sentence represents an unduly modest description of his contribution to the occasion. In a debate in the House of Lords in 1958 its outcome was recalled as follows: 'One or two of us went to see the Home Secretary . . . but we got no change out of him. The ball was passed back to the watch committee and we got no change out of them. I am not saying whether we were right or wrong but I formed then a strong opinion that a chief constable had a privileged position in the British Constitution.' (213 H.L. Deb. col. 34.)

The minutes of the Oxford Watch Committee for 10 September 1936 record that 'The Committee considered a letter received by the Chairman of the Committee from the Hon. Frank Pakenham stating that he must place before the Chairman a serious complaint regarding the conduct of the chief constable . . . and that he had laid a dossier before Sir John Simon who had informed him that the Committee is the proper body to deal with the matter and requesting a hearing by the Committee . . . Mr Pakenham will be informed that the Committee is in possession of the dossier referred to in his letter and are of opinion that no useful purpose could be served by an interview . . .'

the time of the assault or afterwards from the police. Sir John Simon replied that allegations against the conduct of the provincial police fell to be dealt with by the local disciplinary authority. He would submit Pakenham's statement to the chief constable of Oxford for his observations, but the Home Secretary had 'not got the function of making inquiries about police incidents all over the country'.[1]

Attempts were also made to raise this and similar issues in the House of Commons on the Home Office Supply Vote[2] and produced an interesting and protracted dialogue between Members and the Chair. On the estimate for the metropolitan police, Mr Pritt, in moving to reduce the vote by £100, began by alleging that police action in recent times had been 'steadily crushing the ordinary expression of political views' and the conduct of the police, he thought, was such as to give grave reasons to suspect that some influence was at work to make them favourable to Fascists. After further allegations about the behaviour of police in controlling public meetings the Deputy Chairman (Captain Bourne) intervened to say that the Home Office were responsible only for the metropolitan police. Mr Rhys Davies then asked for clarification. 'I have [he said] been on a local authority, and whenever a point of police administration has arisen . . . the Town Clerk has invariably referred us to the Home Office. When we come here to debate this vote we are told that we must go to the watch committee or the standing joint committee.'

To this the Deputy Chairman replied:

'The position as I understand it is this: under Statute the metropolitan police are the direct responsibility of the Home Secretary. It is his responsibility. He can give orders to the metropolitan police and they are bound to obey them. He has responsibility for that. In the case of the provincial police he cannot give orders. The orders to them are given by the statutory authority . . . *They have absolute control over the provincial police* and the Home Secretary cannot give orders to them. The most that he can do is to circularize the local authorities and give them advice . . . The only responsibility of the Home Secretary in respect of the provincial

[1] 314 H.C. Deb. 5s. cols. 223–4.
[2] See 314 H.C. Deb. 5s. col. 1547 *et seq.* (10 July 1936) Mr A. P. Herbert managed to keep within the rules of order by discussing the putative case of a London University professor who might notionally be set upon by Fascist stewards at a public meeting.

police is that he can inspect them and see that they are efficient. If his inspectors find that they are not efficient he can withhold part of the money to be granted, but he cannot withhold a grant because they stop meetings or because they do not stop meetings. That is outside his jurisdiction. He can withhold the grant only if they do not come up to certain standards of efficiency.'[1]

Mr Lansbury nevertheless expressed himself as unable to see why, since they were moving a reduction, they were not entitled to argue that they did not want to vote the money because they were dissatisfied with the manner in which the authorities to whom the money was going were carrying out their duties.

The Deputy Chairman replied that they could discuss the matter only within the limits which under statute they had left to themselves. All they could be concerned with was whether the police were being kept up to an efficient standard. They had taken away any other powers of criticism. Would it not then be in order, Mr Dalton asked, to cite cases of gross inefficiency on the part of the police in provincial areas? Mr Pritt added that the question he wished to raise was indeed one of efficiency. There had, he suggested, been the gravest inefficiency on the part of some highly placed members of the police force in the City of Oxford. Was it not a question of inefficiency if the police were to stand by whilst bodily harm was inflicted and then fail to make the necessary inquiries for a prosecution?

The Deputy Chairman then remarked – somewhat confusingly – that 'The Hon. and learned Member is now criticizing the *efficiency of the police* of Oxford and that is the very thing which I have ruled he cannot do under this Vote'. He added later that the matter 'does not come within the ruling as to efficiency'. The question raised was not one of efficiency within the meaning of the ruling.

Mr Pritt again suggested that he was criticizing the inefficiency of the police in standing by and the Deputy Chairman countered with: 'That is exactly what is not meant by inefficiency in this connection. The only thing that covers efficiency is whether the men are properly drilled, properly trained and properly clothed.'[2]

---

[1] 314 H.C. Deb. 5s. 1554 (italics added).   [2] *Ibid.*, col. 1568.

The exchange continued as follows:

MR ATTLEE Is it not part of the efficient training of a policeman that first of all the police selected should be of sufficient intelligence to know or to be trained to know when a breach of the peace is being perpetrated and therefore if a provincial police force is kept in such a state that they can stand by and see breaches of the peace committed and take no action, surely that is a matter in which we are entitled to complain of the training of that police force and that they are not efficient.

THE DEPUTY CHAIRMAN No, that goes far beyond any ruling which has been given over and over again in this House . . . There have been rulings going back over many years that we cannot discuss in this House the conduct of the provincial police.

MR GALLACHER How is it possible to know whether the police are efficient or not unless by watching how they carry out their duties?

DEPUTY CHAIRMAN The carrying out of their duty is a matter for the watch committee and not for this House.

The rulings given in this debate had two consequences. They helped to confuse the issue about the powers of local police authorities and they solidified a distinction (which as the debate shows cannot be defended with any logical rigour) between the 'efficiency' of the police and their 'operations' or the carrying out of their duty. It has never been quite clear whether this parliamentary distinction between operations and efficiency is one which has been present in the mind of the Home Secretary and his Inspectors. The Home Office memorandum to the Willink Commission defined the duties of the Inspectors of Constabulary as being 'to inspect police forces and advise the Home Secretary as to their *efficiency*'.[1] If efficiency is interpreted as it was in the Commons this should have placed the manner in which police carry out their duties outside the purview of the inspectorate. Yet in the following paragraph of the Home Office memorandum the Inspectors' job is spoken of as being to 'inquire into all aspects of police *administration and operations*' (though it is added that they cannot give directions to chief officers or to watch committees or relieve them of their responsibilities). Again in 1957 when the Select Committee on Estimates took evi-

[1] Cmnd. 1728, Minutes of Evidence, Appendix 11, p. 8.

dence from the Inspectors, one of them said, 'We have come over the years to interpret the function of report upon the efficiency as covering everything from the balance of a recreation fund to the hot water in the bath and the general wellbeing, technical efficiency and above all the integrity and organization of the force.'[1] The force's integrity, it might be thought, is hardly separable from the way in which its duties are carried out. The parliamentary definition of efficiency seemed, in fact, inconsistent with the doctrine that the Secretary of State for Home Affairs is in some sense responsible for law and order throughout the kingdom. This notion pointed towards a distinction in terms of the general and the particular rather than towards a distinction between all operations (both general and particular) on the one hand and logistical adequacy on the other. Something of this former concept seems to have prevailed on occasions when parliamentary questions have been admitted and answered in relation to particular local incidents. In 1957, for example, a question was admitted about the alleged failure of the police throughout the country to prevent the interruption of public transport services during a provincial bus strike.[2] It seems to have been possible also to raise detailed local matters or incidents by asking whether any report had been received of them. For example, a disorder in Bristol in 1934 produced a question to the Home Secretary inquiring whether any report had been received from the local superintendent of police. In reply Sir John Gilmour indicated that he had received such a report and stated its contents.[3] In relation to Scotland questions might be founded upon the provision in the Scottish police legislation, consolidated in 1956, giving to the Secretary of State a statutory right to call for reports from chief constables. For example, on 4 April 1962, the Secretary of State was asked whether he would call for a report from the chief constable of Glasgow about disorder at Ibrox football stadium.

The exact nature of the Home Secretary's responsibility to Parliament even for the metropolitan police[4] has given rise to some apparent divergence of opinion. One Home Office view as to the

[1] H.C. 307 (1958) p. 108.
[2] 574 H.C. Deb. 5s. cols. 600–5.
[3] 291 H.C. Deb. 5s. col. 1122.
[4] See above, Chap. 2.

metropolitan force was that the Secretary of State is responsible for the general policy of the force in the discharge of its duty but that 'he cannot be questioned about ... the discharge by individual police officers of the duties of law enforcement which they perform as officers of the Crown'.[1] This does not seem to square with the practice of the House of Commons or to take adequate account of the fact that the discharge of duties by individual police officers may well raise questions of general policy and public controversy. The Home Office memorandum in fact mentions the inquiries into the Savidge case of 1928 and the Waters inquiry of 1959, both of which arose from the acts of individual police officers, as did the Challenor inquiry and proceedings in 1964. The view of Sir Edward Fellowes, Clerk of the House of Commons, was that in relation to the metropolitan police 'No general limitation can be said to exist at all' as to questions in the House.[2] There has never been a ruling as to whether it would be in order to ask the Home Secretary to instruct the metropolitan police to prosecute or to take other action in a particular case. Sir David Maxwell Fyfe in reply to a question about police activities in relation to parking in 1954 replied that it was not within his province to instruct the police when to deal with offences and when not.[3] The phraseology is ambiguous and it is unclear whether it expresses a view about legal incompetence or administrative impropriety. Matters involving prosecution and particular cases are normally left to the Metropolitan Police Commissioner but there seems no restriction as to the particularity of the lawful orders which the Home Secretary as police authority may issue.[4] Occasionally similar language has been used by the Home Secretary when asked to state the nature of directions issued to the police. On 13 February 1958, for example, Mr R. A. Butler was asked what instructions had been given to the police in the metropolitan area with regard to the leaving of cars outside houses in residential districts. His reply was that it would not be proper for him to

[1] Cmnd. 1728, Minutes of Evidence, Appendix 11, p. 16.

[2] See *ibid.*, Appendix 11, p. 23.   [3] 529 H.C. Deb. 5s. col. 590.

[4] Sir John Moylan (*Scotland Yard and the Metropolitan Police*, 1934, p. 80): 'The Commissioner is ... subject to the directions of the Secretary of State in the execution of all his duties.'

publish the details of operational instructions.[1] The impropriety, it may be suggested, here is clearly not a legal one. It is a ministerial synonym for such adjectives as 'inappropriate' and the question is plainly one of administrative practice and assumed convenience.

The procedural difficulties in the way of raising provincial police questions in the Commons were, until 1964, considerable, not only because of the restricted, though ambiguous responsibilities of the Home Secretary and local authorities, but also because of the procedural rules of the House. The provisions, for example, which govern the raising of matters on the adjournment prevent debate on issues which would necessitate legislation and which are not within the existing administrative competence of the minister involved. For a similar reason Mr Godfrey Lagden was frustrated in April 1958 when he attempted to secure a debate in Committee of Supply on the selection and appointment of chief constables. Though the standing orders provide for the admission of incidental references to legislative action at the Speaker's discretion the view taken by the Chair was that 'the Hon. Member's difficulty is that the control of local police forces and chief constables is in the hands of the local authority. It is a question of considerable controversy whether that should be changed so as to make a Minister in this House responsible for them. That would mean legislation.'[2] The same principle has clearly prevented the discussion of other police matters in the Commons.[3]

Thus, though the procedural restrictions might be avoided on the few occasions when a substantive motion could be debated, Members of Parliament found themselves frequently unable to utilize the most profitable opportunities at question time and on the adjournment to debate police matters arising in the provinces. Citizens who hoped to hear some particular issue ventilated might have the odd experience of hearing it said in the House that Parliament could offer no redress since local authorities were in absolute control of the police and of then discovering that their local

[1] 582 H.C. Deb. 5s. col. 84.   [2] 586 H.C. Deb. 5s. col. 1294.
[3] See the evidence of Mr Godfrey Lagden, M.P., and Dr Donald McI. Johnson, M.P., to the Royal Commission. Cmnd. 1728, Day 22.

representatives and watch committee were in no such position. The situation was particularly irritating for Members whose constituencies lay on the boundaries of the metropolitan area. As the Member for Hornchurch put it, 'Should a constituent of the Members of Parliament of Ilford or Dagenham . . . complain to their Members of Parliament of the actions of a police officer and should on the same day a constituent of mine do the same thing, the Members previously referred to could raise the matter by the method of questions to the Home Secretary, and if dissatisfied with his replies by applying for the adjournment debate, but neither of these methods would be open to me.'[1]

Even inside the metropolitan area members might find that the Home Secretary was unwilling to do anything more than support the decisions in particular cases of the Metropolitan Police Commissioner. It was a censure debate arising out of an episode of this kind which led directly to the appointment of the Royal Commission on the Police of 1960-2. The episode itself was an odd one. It had been alleged in a High Court action that a civil servant whose car had been stopped by a metropolitan police constable had been violently assaulted by him. The facts were never ascertained since the metropolitan police paid into court £300 without admission of liability and the plaintiff took the sum in settlement of his claim. On 5 November 1959 the Home Secretary was asked what disciplinary action was proposed by the Metropolitan Police Commissioner; to what department the constable had been assigned and to what extent this assignment brought him into contact with the public. Mr Butler replied that the Commissioner had decided that no disciplinary proceedings should be taken and that it was not his practice to disclose the disposition of his officers. Mr Gordon Walker reminded the Home Secretary that he was responsible to the House, and Mr Butler replied that he accepted responsibility but was unable to carry the matter further. In a supplementary question Mr Gaitskell suggested that this was not very satisfactory, since there was evidence that this particular officer had been involved in other episodes with the public and that it was surprising that no action had

[1] Cmnd. 1728, Minutes of Evidence, Day 22, p. 1233.

been taken. Could not the Home Secretary at least give the reasons for his decision? To this the Home Secretary returned the answer that it was a matter of discretion; that there were a great variety of facts in the case and that the Commissioner had been into them; that he had given all the relevant facts that he knew to the House, and that he must accept responsibility.[1]

As a demonstration of parliamentary accountability in action this may well have struck Members as lacking in conviction. A censure motion was put down[2] and in the course of his reply for the Government on 18 November, Mr Butler announced the decision to set up a Royal Commission. One of its members – Mr Leslie Hale – later had a phrase for it. It was, he said, 'appointed in one of those gay, irresponsible, but long premeditated afterthoughts for which the right hon. Gentleman, the then Home Secretary, was famous'.

[1] 612 H.C. Deb. 5s. cols. 1196-9.   [2] 613 H.C. Deb. 5s. cols. 1239-1303.

5 The Evidence to the Royal Commission

IN JANUARY 1961 THE ROYAL COMMISSION UNDER SIR HENRY Willink began hearing evidence. Its major terms of reference were 'To review the constitutional position of the police throughout Great Britain, the arrangements for their control and administration and in particular to consider (1) the constitution and functions of local police authorities; (2) the status and accountability of members of police forces, including chief officers of police; (3) the relationship of the police with the public and the means of ensuring that complaints by the public against the police are effectively dealt with.' In the 1400 pages of memoranda and proceedings, there is a wealth of material to fascinate students of British government and, for that matter, British psychology. The memoranda ranged from one end of the spectrum of social administration to the other. The Association of Scottish Police Superintendents, for example, prefaced their evidence with some reflections on the definition of dynamic democracy and the nature of happiness. Other witnesses were more anxious to discuss the depth of kitchen sinks in police houses. In the intermediate range of problems two different kinds of division of opinion were seen to exist amongst those who gave evidence. There was a division of opinion similar to that which appeared before the Franks Committee between those who favour more control of and avenues for complaint against executive discretion and those who are satisfied with the existing forms of accountability. There was another and rather different division of opinion between advocates of regionalization or nationalization of police forces and those who insisted upon the essentially local nature

58

of police services. On this second question what might be called the conservative view was represented by the local authority associations and the chief constables (the chief constable of Lancashire dissenting). The radicals and nationalizers included the Inns of Court Conservative and Unionist Society, the Law Society, the Magistrates·Association and the English, Welsh and Scottish Police Federations. On accountability as distinct from organization the alliances were different. On this topic – in particular the part to be played by watch committees and county standing joint committees in the supervision of police operations, appointments and discipline – the chief constables and local authorities parted company.

A NATIONAL FORCE

Outright nationalization of the police appeared to be unpopular as a concept. Even those who wanted it did not want to call it by the name. The proposals which came nearest in effect to nationalization were those of the Law Society. They recommended that control by local police authorities should be abolished and that a Central Police Commission directly responsible to Parliament should be appointed. Its membership, it was suggested, should be drawn from the ranks of present or ex-chief constables with each region of England and Wales represented by a Commissioner who had served as a chief officer in that region. In addition there should be a National Advisory and Consultative Committee with similar local committees on a county basis and the title 'Royal Constabulary' or 'Her Majesty's Constabulary' should be adopted. Neither the financial nor the constitutional details of this scheme were worked out with any great thoroughness. The Law Society's witnesses insisted that they were not advocating a national force since existing chief officers were to remain in control of local forces with their existing responsibilities at common law unimpaired, and the idea of the Commission was 'merely to co-ordinate'. Taken at its face value such a Commission seemed to be little more than a complicated extension of the Home Office. If on the other hand it was to be assumed that a Commission might work on the analogy of a nationalized industry board its executive powers would have had to go further into day-to-day administration than co-ordinating or advising and brooding about policy.

Similar problems were implicit, of course, in any scheme for nationalizing, rationalizing or regionalizing forces. As between regionalization or 'countyization' and the existing structure the arguments were predominantly about efficiency rather than constitutional principle. Nobody suggested that the liberties of Englishmen might be frittered away by transferring city police files across the road to the county headquarters. Rather was it that one school of thought believed (and believes) that efficiency can only be achieved by larger organizations and economies of scale. The other faction held that greater efficiency could be achieved without wholesale reorganization of units by co-operation, by some measure of amalgamation and by sharing of services. The confrontation of these viewpoints came out most clearly in the majority and minority memoranda of the Association of Chief Police Officers. Of the 125 provincial police forces in England and Wales, eleven were stated to have establishments of more than 1000. Fifty-six forces or almost half the total had an establishment of less than 250. Colonel T. E. St Johnston, chief constable of Lancashire, argued in a brisk minority memorandum that forces of this size must be uneconomic and relatively inefficient. They were, he suggested, too small to provide good promotion incentives, to give potentially good officers varied experience or to afford specialized technical equipment such as helicopters or small fixed-wing light aircraft. At the same time, he claimed, crime investigation on a regional basis might be hindered by possible failure of co-operation or reluctance of local forces to give up control of their independent communications schemes. (A criminal might 'steal a car in North Cheshire and travel to Rochdale in less than one hour, during which time he could pass through six different police areas all of which have different wireless frequencies'.) Many of these criticisms were also made by the Inns of Court Conservative Society's memorandum – in particular the insufficient attractiveness of police service as now organized to entrants with advanced educational qualifications. Eleven police regions were suggested. Colonel Johnston's scheme envisaged twenty.

None of these arguments convinced the majority of chief constables, or the Association of Municipal Corporations or the County Councils Association. The chief constables' watchwords were mutual aid and common services. They emphasized that training, promotion examinations, wireless maintenance and forensic science laboratories were paid for out of the Common Services Fund to which all forces contribute on a per capita basis. Other forms of specialist training such as driving and detective courses could, they suggested, be financed in the same way and the existing sharing of expenditure on regional criminal record offices could provide a model for the provision of expensive technical equipment. Co-operation and consultation through the thrice-yearly Central Conference and District Conferences they thought to be adequate. Nor did communication difficulties worry them. The Scottish chief constables mentioned as one of the incidental advantages of Scottish administration that their forces were equipped with special common wavelength link sets. These (if not Procurators Fiscal) might, it was implied, conceivably work in Lancashire.

Little discussion took place on two important questions: first the effect of administrative surgery on local government; and secondly the implications of regional or central commissioners for parliamentary responsibility. The nationalized industry model with the Minister entitled to decline questions on day-to-day matters obviously provided an analogy for those who wished accountability to be transferred away from the local representative level. But did they envisage that local authorities and electorates should retain some opportunities for querying and informing themselves about the local activities of the regional or royal constabulary? If so, how? These questions were not seriously discussed before the Royal Commission at all. Nobody who has read the evidence could possibly emerge believing that the organizational issue had been thoroughly thrashed out by the witnesses. The detail was too scanty and the familiar homely note of grinding axes too pervasive.

COMPLAINTS

Some useful statistics about complaints against the police appeared in the evidence to the Commission. The record of disciplinary offences compiled annually by H.M. Inspectors of Constabulary, for example, showed that during the 1950s the figure fluctuated between about 700 and 1400. Over the same period the number of police constables required to resign or dismissed averaged about 60 per annum. This could not be called a large number. The Metropolitan Police Commissioner also supplied some figures relating to complaints against the police in the London area. In 1959 there were 1700[1] of which 200 were regarded as substantiated. Statistics collected over the years do not, of course, permit any direct inferences about changes in police behaviour towards the public. They tend, for example, to increase with increases in the total number of police employed and with more elaborate procedures for recording and dealing with complaints. The social psychology of a middle-class society was also alleged by some witnesses to have augmented the national propensity to complain. 'The days', Sir Joseph Simpson wrote, 'when people were prepared to accept the directions of a policeman without question are gone.' Again it was suggested that isolated incidents widely covered by the press might affect the figures for a particular year. The 'Thurso boy' case which led to the tribunal of inquiry into the Waters allegations in 1959 was followed, according to the Commissioner's figures, by a marked increase in the number of accusations of assault.

Some public complaints obviously relate to and vary with legislative policies which the police have to carry out, rather than police initiative as such. The Road Traffic Acts account for a good deal. In the metropolis in fact the largest category of complainers appears to be composed of car, bus and taxicab drivers who have been reported for offences, and prisoners already in custody or in gaol. Neither situation, admittedly, is conducive to a cool appreciation of the difference between legislative and executive responsibilities.

[1] Figures recently given for 1963 and 1938 show that the number of complaints in those years was 1,889 and 1,866 respectively.

The metropolitan procedure for handling complaints was set out in detail. (They averaged out at one complaint for every 20,000 hours of police duty, which is a reasonable enough score and possibly a record for any metropolitan area. It would be interesting to see some comparative figures for, say, Paris and Denver, Colorado.) It was stated that if it was apparent from a complaint that a breach of discipline had occurred the formal procedure laid down under the discipline regulations was used. In less clear or serious cases statements might be taken informally from a complainant. He would first be asked if he were willing to leave the matter in the hands of the Commissioner, and it would usually be possible to tell him the result of the complaint though not the details of any disciplinary action.

Many witnesses who appeared before the Commission were dissatisfied with this system and wanted some or all complaints to be handled by an independent person or tribunal. The National Council for Civil Liberties, for example, made a number of allegations about police behaviour, mainly in relation to the handling of political demonstrations in London. Their account of the attention which in their experience was given to individual complainants did not entirely tally with that set out in the Commissioner's memorandum. They remarked that there was no normally understood procedure for registering a complaint at a police station. They drew attention to the difficulty of identifying senior police officers who wear no numbers. They complained that the Home Secretary would not answer letters about the metropolitan police except by a brief reply that the Commissioner was responsible for order and that the complaint had been passed to him.

The arrangements for considering complaints were in fact thought unsatisfactory by both Labour and Conservative lawyers, by the Law Society and the Faculty of Advocates and much of their evidence was directed to the question whether complaints procedures could be formalized without placing an undue burden on the police. The Faculty of Advocates' suggestion was that a panel of investigating officers drawn from various forces should be responsible to the Chief Inspector of Constabulary in Scotland. The Law

Society wanted a system of independent tribunals to review a chief constable's decision if a complainant should prove dissatisfied with it. One difficulty of any such review system, which was much canvassed before the Commission, was that constables could find themselves placed in jeopardy twice over, once within the force and again before a tribunal, with the further possibility, in some cases, of legal action in the courts.

ACCOUNTABILITY

In the matter of civil liability towards persons injured by the act or default of the police there was a surprising unanimity amongst the majority of those who gave evidence that it would not be right to make police authorities vicariously liable in tort or to extend the provisions of the Crown Proceedings Act to the police. The Commission may have been tempted to believe that any proposal so emphatically and simultaneously denounced by chief constables, magistrates, local authorities and the Home Office cannot have been completely without merit, and there were in fact some potential inconsistencies in the arguments about police psychology stressed by many witnesses. It was suggested, for example (in the Law Society's memorandum), that personal liability is a necessary restraint upon the police and that without it a constable might act without sufficient consideration or caution. Yet it was argued by other witnesses that a constable could not carry out his duties effectively if on every occasion on which he had to act he had to consider the risk of an action being brought against him. Moreover, it was said, for at least thirty years the Police Federation had devoted itself to securing that in practice police authorities should stand behind the police by meeting the costs of any proceedings brought against a constable in respect of an action taken in good faith in the intended execution of his duty.

The practice had been in fact generally adopted, though not on any uniform basis. Various difficulties seemingly arose from it. The metropolitan police, according to the Home Office memorandum, offered the services of a solicitor as soon as proceedings are instituted but without deciding until after the hearing whether any damages awarded would be met from the Metropolitan Police Fund. The Oaksey Committee noted in 1948 that in Scotland a decision was made about financial support by the police authority immediately and not at the end of proceedings. They recommended the Scottish system, but a Police Federation inquiry in 1960 suggested that only a handful of forces in England and Wales had adopted the Oaksey Committee's view.

If the police have been on the whole protected against the financial rigour of their personal liability the position of the citizen has not necessarily been so happy. It can have been little consolation to him to know that whether there would be money to meet his claim would depend upon whether a defendant policeman was acting reasonably in the eye of the police authority. Redress is equally necessary when a possibly impecunious defendant has acted unreasonably and may for that very reason not be financially supported.

The simplest remedy would have been to make police authorities vicariously liable for the wrongful acts of police. This course, however, would have required statutory modification of the principle laid down in *Fisher v. Oldham Corporation*. It was not likely to be favoured by anyone who believed that to make the police into 'servants' of watch committees and standing joint committees for this purpose would undermine their constitutional independence in general.

On the constitutional question sharp differences of opinion arose between the local authorities on the one hand and the Home Office and police view on the other. The Association of Municipal Corporations argued strongly that *Fisher v. Oldham* did not dictate any conclusion about the supervisory powers of watch committees over their police forces.

On this point the evidence given about the position of the police in Scotland offered some interesting comparisons. Though the rule as to civil liability is the same the police do not have exactly the same ambit of independent discretion as has been claimed in England and Wales. In the consolidating Police (Scotland) Act of 1956, it was provided that in the investigation of offences (since the police do not prosecute) chief constables should comply with the instructions of the appropriate prosecutor. These lawful instructions were referred to in the Act (which also preserved and declared the powers of burgh magistrates to give lawful instructions to the police 'whether general or as respects any particular case'). Such instructions, though infrequent, might be important. In evidence the regulation of procession routes was mentioned as a subject for directions, but strikes and political disorders were suggested as other possible occasions. A further provision incorporated in the Scottish Act was the duty of chief constables to submit whenever required a report to the police authority, the magistrates, sheriff or the Secretary of State on 'matters connected with the policing of the area'. It was not at all clear that 'policing' here was restricted to questions of finance and efficiency in the narrow sense.

As to England and Wales the views of the Association of Chief Police Officers were understandably inclined in the direction of police autonomy. Their memorandum of evidence explained that the constitutional position of chief constables was in general the same as that of the latest joined recruit and that a police authority could not direct a chief constable as to the manner in which he should carry out the enforcement of the law any more than they could direct a particular constable as to the exercise of his individual authority. These two operations were implicitly equated and there was no attempt to distinguish between particular acts of law enforcement and general policies which might be adopted in policing an area. Not only was it held in the memorandum that police authorities might give no instructions but even the right to give advice was held to be restricted to 'the sphere of general administration' (though that sphere was not defined). Decisions might have to be made by chief constables in such matters as 'racial disturbances, outbreaks of disorderly behaviour by irresponsible sections of the public, political demonstrations and marches, strikes arousing serious clashes of feeling between opposing sides, a spate of serious crime resulting in widespread concern and sometimes physical fear'. But 'apart from the advice of his senior officers *there is no authority to whom a chief constable can turn in matters of this kind; no committee to consult* and frequently very little time in which to make a most vital decision'.[1]

---

[1] Cmnd. 1728. Minutes of Evidence, Day 15, p. 851 (italics added).

The memorandum mentions as a possible criticism of the position outlined that chief constables may seem not to be answerable to anybody for the exercise of their powers and meets it by suggesting that they are answerable to the law and the courts in the event of wrongful action being taken. The eventualities mentioned however are plainly not such that it would make sense to speak of the chief constable being answerable to 'the law' for the way in which he carried out his operations. There would be a number of alternative ways of tackling disorderly behaviour or racial disturbance which would all be within the law and which might yet be alleged to be administratively or morally wrong. No question would arise of the courts enforcing responsibility for the policies followed as distinct from any wrongful (in the sense of illegal) acts which might happen to be carried out in the course of them. The assertion that 'provincial police officers . . . are responsible to the courts and not to the central or local government'[1] makes therefore a misleading point in the context of a false alternative. The oral evidence given by the representatives of the Chief Constables' Association did not entirely clarify the points made in the memorandum about consultation. Mr S. Lawrence and Mr E. J. Dodd, chief constables of Kingston-upon-Hull and Birmingham,[2] were asked whether they were saying that a watch committee might not say to a chief constable that he was, for example, being unduly rough with fascists or taking insufficient notice of processions:

CHAIRMAN Are you saying that the watch committee cannot even discuss that sort of thing?

MR LAWRENCE We are not saying that, Sir.

MR DODD We are not saying that at all, Sir. We are saying that the chief constable will listen to any opinions that are given . . . but we do deny the right of a police authority or of any other body to instruct the chief constable as to the way in which his duty should be performed.

CHAIRMAN . . . Supposing there was a pub in the city where there was continual disturbance, where teenagers were very troublesome or there was a colour problem or something of that sort, might he not

[1] *Ibid.*, p. 859.
[2] Mr (now Sir Edward) Dodd subsequently became Chief Inspector of Constabulary.

and would he not be wise to have consultations of an informal kind with the watch committee as elected representatives of the city in question as to how this could be helpfully dealt with?

MR DODD I can see no objection to that and in fact that does now take place.

SIR IAN JACOB . . . Take the case in a borough or city where the watch committee feels that some particular form of criminal activity is prevalent; would you consider that a watch committee could say to the chief constable – 'We now want you to make a special effort for the next year to deal with this particular thing, if necessary at the expense of something else'?

MR DODD No, I would not go as far as that, Sir. I think the watch committee would be perfectly entitled to draw the chief constable's attention to any particular police problem that has arisen within their area and then leave it to the good sense of the chief constable . . .[1]

The Home Office's memorandum of evidence, like that of the chief constables, suggested that the existing position of constables subjected them to 'the control of the law', that the position was basically sound and that it should not be disturbed. The complex question of relations between police authority and chief constable was disposed of succinctly in a paragraph of eight lines. It began:

The question may be asked whether there is any effective safeguard against the failure of a chief officer to enforce the law impartially or to initiate disciplinary proceedings in suitable cases. The broad answer is that if a chief officer were failing in his duty in these respects, the efficiency of the force would be in question and the police authority would have a duty to take action.[2]

The answer may be broad but it is hardly satisfactory. It does not seem to be entirely consistent with the distinction implicit in the chief constables' evidence between administrative efficiency conceded to be within the police authority's jurisdiction and all matters of law enforcement alleged to be outside it. And even on a wider understanding of efficiency the Home Office formula would have to

[1] Day 15, p. 874.
[2] See Minutes of Evidence, Appendix II. *Selection of further evidence submitted which was not made the basis of oral examination*, p. 15.

68

meet the criticism that some control might be felt necessary over policies whose pursuit could not be called 'inefficient' on a particular occasion or be thought in any way to be symptomatic of a general breakdown of efficiency in the force.

The fullest debate on this central issue (to which one would not assume on the evidence of its memorandum that the Home Office had ever devoted any thought) took place in the examination of the witnesses who appeared on behalf of the Association of Municipal Corporations. In its memorandum the Association suggested that police authorities did and should have power to do whatever seemed to them necessary to police their area efficiently, so far as statute, regulation or common law did not derogate from that power. 'Efficiency' meant 'efficiency in enforcing the law, diligently, temperately and equitably'. The general proposition that law enforcement even in its wider aspects was not subject to the surveillance of the police authority could not be inferred from *Fisher's* case. The most substantial limitation of the police authority's discretion was that it was not empowered to interfere in the application of the criminal law in particular cases. Apart from that, the delegation by the watch committee of executive control of the force to the chief constable was a matter not of law but of good administrative practive. But there was nothing in law to prevent their giving him even instructions in certain cases. There might be circumstances in which the police authority was dissatisfied with the general manner in which the police were keeping the peace:

> We think that it would be their right and duty to require the chief constable to take steps to enforce the law more vigorously in order to preserve the peace. Similarly, if the watch committee formed the view that their force had acted with unnecessary violence in dealing with a political demonstration we think that they would be *intra vires* in requiring the chief constable to use gentler methods in future; and again if the watch committee were of opinion that the chief constable was prejudiced against a particular group or element of the community we think that it would be their duty to say so and to require him to mend his ways.[1]

[1] Days 11–12, pp. 629–31.

These views were defended orally before the Royal Commission, where the extent to which the 'disposition of the force' came within the police authority's jurisdiction was debated at length. Sir Harold Banwell and other local authority representatives argued that the Commission should discount the view of the Oaksey Committee (cited by the Chief Constables' Association) that 'the police authority have no right to give the chief constable orders about the disposition of the force or the way in which police duties should be carried out'.[1] Sir Harold Banwell, by way of rebuttal, cited an example:

If a chief constable was ridiculous enough to decide he would put no constables on night duty, then I cannot believe that the police authority could escape the responsibility of telling him he had got to do it. I do not for one moment think they would be foolish enough to tell him how many he was to put or how to spread them out . . . This is all a question of degree . . . it is the right and duty of the police authority to tell him what to do, not in detail but in general.

Alderman Hoy (chairman of the Association's Police Committee) suggested a similar illustration:

If, for example, your chief constable would not employ modern aids, would not have motor cars, I think it would be the watch committee's duty to say: we will have them and you will use them to combat crime.

He added:

We are not seeking to be able to tell the chief constable; you must arrest so and so; we do not want those powers. [But] There must be some accountability. We must have that reserve of power which would be able to call upon a chief constable to give an account of his stewardship or his general behaviour or management.

Other local representatives listed for the Commission the matters discussed by watch committees in their areas. Councillor Langton (of Manchester) said:

The chief constable comes every month to the watch committee with his report and discusses with his watch committee the details of every conceivable aspect of police administration. He does not discuss with us an

[1] *Report of the Committee on Police Conditions of Service*, Pt II, 1949 (Cmd. 7831), para. 185.

individual crime, but he will discuss with us crime generally, what he means to do with crime generally. Sometimes his demands are extravagant and sometimes they are reasonable. We discuss these problems with him; there is a great deal of discussion.[1]

In short the representatives of the borough police authorities rejected the distinction between 'efficiency' on the one hand and 'law enforcement', 'operations' and 'disposition of forces' on the other. They conceded that it was obviously not permissible to give such instructions to a chief constable as would result in a breach of the general law and they agreed that it was administratively undesirable that there should be instructions or interference with either the technical details of law enforcement or with the institution of individual prosecutions.

Little detailed discussion of these matters is to be found in any of the other evidence submitted to the Commission. There is however in the memorandum written by Professor E. C. S. Wade an interesting paragraph in which the relations between police and police authorities are discussed. Professor Wade suggests that confusion about the independence of the police in enforcing the law has arisen because it has been insufficiently realized that the maintenance of public order is an executive function which strictly speaking is everybody's business but which has become for the most part the monopoly of the police. Freedom from outside interference properly attaches only to judicial functions, 'But as a matter of strict law anyone can normally start a prosecution on his own initiative and therefore there is nothing exceptional in a local police authority requiring the police to carry out this duty since each has an equal responsibility for it. There can I think be little ground in law for the assumption that the discretion exercised by a chief constable is peculiar to himself. No doubt it is wholly desirable that in practice there should be no interference with his discretion, particularly with regard to prosecutions ... But this does not absolve the police authority from responsibility for enforcement of the law.' Thus, Professor Wade continued, there is no reason why a watch committee should not instruct a chief constable to increase his efforts to

[1] Days 11-12 (quotations from pp. 668-72).

71

suppress certain categories of crime. In relation to questions where for example excessive force had been alleged against the police it would be reasonable for the watch committee to consider unnecessary force as a breach of discipline. He concludes: 'The suggestion that it would be *ultra vires* for the watch committee to give orders in such circumstances to its chief constable seems to me to be untenable.'[1]

Clearly, the thesis advanced by the municipal local authorities and that supported by the chief constables cannot be reconciled. Whatever organizational matters were to occupy the attention of the Royal Commission the question of constitutional status and accountability remained central. The relation of police to political or representative authority has to be determined whether the latter is to be a local committee, a regional commissioner or a nationalized grand panjandrum. The question had never been adequately examined or resolved by any earlier Royal Commission. It was therefore a matter of both academic interest and practical urgency to see what the Willink Commission would make of it.

[1] Minutes of Evidence, Appendix II, pp. 33-4.

6 The Commission's Report

THE TERMS OF REFERENCE GIVEN TO SIR HENRY WILLINK WERE wide-ranging. There were to be recommendations on police salaries, on status and accountability, on police organization and on relations with the public. So the Commission's job was a large one. Perhaps it was too large. It is a considerable way from pay to public relations via the Road Traffic Acts, nineteenth-century administrative history and some complicated pieces of constitutional law. Sir Henry and his men had to be in turn economists, sociologists and historians. There were, naturally, no economists, sociologists or historians on the Commission.

Yet widely as the inquiry ranged it seems odd in retrospect that some important topics were not covered. Police powers of arrest, search and inquiry which had not been examined since 1929 were thought to be outside the terms of reference. So also was prosecution policy and its uniformity or lack of uniformity, though it could hardly be supposed irrelevant to the question of police relations with the public. Two other topics which remained largely unexamined were parliamentary accountability for police activities and the day-to-day working of the Home Office's relations with local authorities. Nor were any efforts made to elaborate specific morals which might be drawn from the episodes in Glamorgan, Brighton, Nottingham, Thurso and London, which led up to the appointment of the Royal Commission. Little or nothing, at any rate, on these topics appears in the Report. Home Office witnesses gave evidence, but their evidence does not form part of the published minutes. Nor does that of the four ex-Home Secretaries whose views were sought. Why not? Can every word of it have been confidential? Can Mr Chuter Ede, Lord Morrison and Viscounts Tenby and Kilmuir have been sitting on such a mine of scandalous and embarrassing information that the lieges must hear none of it? Was there no word that could be breathed in public by Mr R. A. Butler? Did the Commission and the Home Office really ask themselves which parts of the world would fall in pieces if the views of Sir Charles Cunningham and Captain Athelstan Popkess were recorded in print?

RECOMMENDATIONS

The major conclusions of the Report may be summarized as follows:
Chief constables should be subject to more effective supervision, but there should be no change in the legal status of police officers of any rank (Recommendations 4 and 5)

The legal responsibility for the efficient policing of an area should be transferred to the Secretary of State (Recommendation 12)

Chief constables should submit annual reports on the policing of their areas (Recommendation 16)

The right of a member of a local council to ask questions of a chairman of a police authority should be recognized on the understanding that there would be no obligation to reply if this would be contrary to law or the public interest (Recommendation 17)

Police authorities should continue to be responsible for the appointment of chief constables subject to the approval of the Secretary of State. In general chief constables should be appointed from another force and this should be made a condition of appointment by regulation after seven years (Recommendation 18)

The powers to suspend and dismiss chief constables and deputies under the County Police Act 1839 and the Municipal Corporations Act 1882 should be repealed (Recommendation 21)

The powers of watch committees in relation to appointment, promotion and discipline of subordinate ranks should be transferred to the chief constable (Recommendation 24)

Police authorities should be made liable for the wrongful acts of police officers (Recommendation 28)

74

Police authorities in England and Wales should include co-opted justices as one third of their membership (Recommendation 31)

The Home Secretary and Secretary of State for Scotland, having statutory responsibility for the efficiency of the police, should have power to call for reports from chief constables on matters connected with the policing of their areas. The Secretaries of State should be responsible for securing that police authorities carry out their duties, that each separate force is efficient, that groups of forces collaborate efficiently and that proper ancillary services are provided. (Recommendations 40, 41 and 69)

A chief inspector of constabulary for Great Britain should be appointed with a central unit for planning and research and an increase in the inspectorate from five to eight (Recommendations 43–5)

The 'optimum' size of a force should be at least five hundred (Recommendation 53)

An expert working party should review police areas as a basis for the amalgamation of police forces (Recommendation 56)

The minimum qualifying period for promotion to sergeant should be reduced from five to three years (Recommendation 63)

Inspectors and police authorities should have a duty to satisfy themselves that complaints were properly dealt with and have the right to inspect complaints books in which all complaints should be recorded. There should be a standard leaflet on complaints procedure; a letter from a senior officer should notify the result of each complaint and complainants should be entitled to attend disciplinary hearings and put questions (Recommendations 96–108)

Three members of the Commission suggested the appointment of a Complaints Commissioner and Dr A. L. Goodhart in a dissenting report argued the case for a national police force (see below, p. 151).

STATUS AND ACCOUNTABILITY

The Report begins by posing a question in the following form: How can the police be an impartial force in the body politic and yet be subject to a degree of control by persons who are not required to be impartial? How in other words can an impartial body be under any degree of control by a political body without prejudicing its impartiality? This question with its implicit analogy between 'partiality' and politics is misleading. For one thing it confuses 'politics' and 'party politics'. Many decisions are made 'politically' in the sense that they have an impact on society and are made according to some discretionary policy rather than by fixed rules, but they need not thereby be either partisan in the party sense or biased against individuals. When we say that the police must be impartial we mean that they must apply rules of law without exceptions or favours for particular individuals or parties; but in this sense it is not true that political representatives on police authorities are 'not required to be impartial'. In so far as there are clear rules of action everybody must be impartial. In so far as there is discretion to act or discretion as to the manner of acting or applying rules, then everybody's judgment, including that of the police, is political or policy judgment. The Commission recognize this when they speak of 'police policies in matters which . . . concern the public interest' (para. 90). But having stated the problem they skirt carefully around it and fail to confront the question of accountability which it raises.

It was the Scottish system of police administration which provided the Commission with the notion of reports to police authorities and to the Secretary of State. In some ways constabulary duties had been more clearly defined in Scotland than in England and Wales. They were framed in the Police (Scotland) Act of 1956 as being to guard, patrol and watch so as to prevent the commission of offences, to preserve order and to protect life and property. In any conceptual classification of activities these could plausibly be called executive or administrative activities in which police authorities responsible by statute for policing their areas might without constitutional impropriety claim a measure of direction and control. In discussing this question the Royal Commission seem to have accepted the view that the constitutional issue and the civil liability issue are separable since they recommended that police authorities might safely (despite the reasoning of McCardie J.) be made liable for the wrongful acts of constables. But they did not follow through the implications of separating the two issues of tort liability and constitutional relationship between police and police authorities. Having in effect rejected the major conclusion of the *Fisher* case they remark that the legal status of constables is beyond doubt – though their own reasoning has thrown doubt on it. They say further that, though in many ways anomalous, the view usually taken of this status is appropriate and need not be altered. They then go on to indicate a number of ways in which the relationship between police and watch committees is inappropriate. They distinguish (in a way which the traditional doctrine never did) between, on the one hand prosecution and law enforcement in particular cases and on the other hand different aspects of enforcement. This is roughly the distinction which was urged in the Municipal Corporations' evidence and which disputed the conclusions usually drawn from *Fisher v. Oldham Corporation*. The Commission implicitly conceded, therefore, that the extreme view of police independence advanced by the majority of witnesses could not be justified. General policies relating to the disposition of forces, the handling of political demonstrations or processions, traffic matters and a number of other activities are not such, they acknowledged, as to require the immunity from external influence that is generally thought necessary in regard to the enforcement of the law in particular cases (para. 91). In this area, they said, a chief constable was not ordinarily brought to account though it is an area which is properly the concern of a representative body (para. 88). In the metropolitan force, the report added, methods of policing and disposition of forces could be and frequently were challenged and debated in the House of Commons and this ought to be possible in the case of provincial forces by local debate and question.

Paradoxically the Commission's suggestions seemed to do little to make this possible. For under the scheme proposed, the responsibilities for efficient policing vested in local representative bodies should, it was suggested, disappear and be statutorily conferred on the Secretary of State. Nothing further was said in the report about local 'challenge' to 'police policies'. In exchange, the suggestion of a police duty to supply reports was offered, but their scope and contents were left vague and the question of accountability remained unclarified.

77

THE PROPOSED REDISTRIBUTION OF RESPONSIBILITY

Two somewhat curious arguments were offered by the Report as reasons for removing responsibilities for efficient policing from local authorities. First it was said that a well-intentioned local authority acting with a full sense of responsibility is in a dilemma in that it may seek to exercise either too much control over the police or too little, and this, it was suggested, raised the question whether the efficiency of policing was a necessary concern of local government. But the way out of this dilemma, if it is one, is plain enough. Why must it be the case that control is too little or too much rather than the right amount and for the right purposes; and why should the possible difficulties of striking this balance suggest in itself that local government is incompetent to strike it?

Another argument ran as follows. The present partnership between local and central government in administering the police failed to maintain police pay at an adequate level sufficient to give the police a sense of fair play or to maintain the strength of the force. A system of control which allowed the situation to deteriorate to this extent must itself be called in question (para. 132). There must be many besides nurses and civil servants who might stand that thesis on its head and make equally good use of it.

The explanation of the transfer of local authority responsibility which the Commission favoured contained a number of obscurities. The Home Secretary was to become in some sense the 'police authority' for the whole country though local authorities seemed still to be referred to as 'police authorities'. Though it was said that they were no longer to be charged with responsibility for the efficient policing of their areas their duties were still defined as those of providing an 'adequate' police force properly equipped and administered; secondly constituting a body of local citizens interested in the maintenance of law and order and concerned with the local standing and well-being of the police; thirdly disciplining and removing senior officers; and fourthly fostering good relations between police and public. On a minimal interpretation these duties might come down to what could be dubbed 'paying, preaching and

78

public relations'. But everything here depends on the meaning of words like 'adequate' (numerically?), 'interested' and 'concerned'. These words are hopelessly vague in this context. So is 'properly administered'. That the administration of an organization, for example, does not include the way in which its units are disposed or carry out their duties would be a surprising notion to anyone professionally concerned with either public or private administration. Equally ambiguous as usual was 'efficiency'. The Report in fact seemed to waver between the broad and the anomalously narrow sense of efficiency according to the requirements of the argument. It was asserted for example that the present situation was unsatisfactory in that police authorities appeared to have responsibilities for the efficient policing of their areas and yet have no technical competence in the matter (para. 157). Here the sense implied seemed to be a wide one – the authority, it was implied, has no skill in criminal detection or knowledge of the best methods of keeping order. But elsewhere 'efficiency' of policing (as contrasted with police operations) seemed to mean such things as bookkeeping, paying out money and maintaining recruitment. In that sense the proposition mentioned is obviously untrue. In the wider sense it still needs to be shown rather than asserted that lack of expertise in the operational and technical aspects of policing is crucial. After all, members of local authorities have no technical competence in planning towns, disposing of sewage or cooking school meals.

A matter which was not entirely clear was whether, when the local authority had lost its responsibility for efficient policing, the reports which it had a right to call for from the local police covered efficiency in its widest sense. It was proposed that the chief constable should have the right of appeal to the Home Secretary in relation to any particular request for a report, but it was not stated, even in the most general way, what types of request would justify an appeal, or on what principles the Home Secretary should make his determination (though it was suggested that the form and scope of annual reports should be prescribed by regulation). The question of principle raised by the Nottingham episode remained something which the Commission did not choose to resolve.

LOCAL AUTHORITY POWERS

The powers of local authorities in their altered form as proposed by the Report could be summarized as follows:

First, they would have a right to put questions to the chairman of the watch committee; but what this would be worth would depend on the chairman's interpretation of the scope of the authority's responsibilities. The authority would lose to the chief constable its power of appointing, disciplining and promoting subordinate ranks, along with its existing power to dismiss chief constables for 'unfitness' under the Municipal Corporations Act of 1882, and the right to appoint members of the watch committee to constitute the tribunal required under the Discipline Regulations for hearing a charge against a chief constable.

Secondly, the local authority should acquire a power to retire a chief constable without the necessity of passing a resolution referring to inefficiency (with an appeal to the Home Secretary). This power was not intended to cover action based on dissatisfaction with what was described as 'a chief constable's command over the force or his enforcement of the law' (para. 181), since power in this field was to rest with the Secretary of State (a wide use of the concept of efficiency), though he would act through the police authority and they might take an initiative by presenting their views to him or to the inspector.

Thirdly, the authority should acquire a legal responsibility for the acts of the police (whom it would not have appointed nor be able to discipline or control).

Fourthly, they should take on certain rights and duties in the complaints field.

COMPLAINTS

Throughout the debate about complaints against the police there can be seen a distinction between two kinds of grievance though one may overlap with the other. On the one hand there is the complaint which in essence involves a disciplinary offence by a single constable or several constables and on the other there is the larger-scale complaint about the general conduct of the police on a particular occasion or the orders given by senior officers. This distinction was made by the three commissioners who proposed a police 'ombudsman' or 'Commissioner of Rights' (and who also wanted this official to act as an appellate authority from the chief constable for minor cases also).

With the wider type of complaint where the reputation and prestige of the force is at stake there seemed much to be said for an impartial procedure less cumbersome than the 1921 Tribunals of Inquiry (Evidence) Act. Given that there is a need for a public independent forum the 'ombudsman' supporters did not seem, in one way, to go far enough. Their recommendation was that there should be three limited findings: 'No cause for criticism', 'A minor error of judgment' and 'A matter for disciplinary or court proceedings'. Such truncated findings seem objectionable in principle. There is surely a legitimate public interest in knowing what lay behind the complaint and the behaviour in question. Should not the public be told what ought to have been done that was not done, and if there was no cause for complaint, why the investigator thought there was no cause for it? Why should this particular tribunal not give its reasons? The minority report suggested that the names of individual police officers should not be given in the Commissioner's reports. This precaution might well have suggested itself to the Royal Commission when it was reviewing the police report on the Trafalgar Square complaints about police behaviour in September 1961. The Home Office evaded the issue of publication by passing the question to the Royal Commission. The Commission did not say why the report should not be published, but merely repeated the ministerial assurance that normal complaints procedures were 'soundly and properly followed'. Some samples of the findings and argument of those investigating the complaints might have allowed the public to judge for itself of their quality. Names could easily have been deleted. It would have been well worth the space devoted to the Royal Commission's social survey on the relations between police and public.[1]

[1] For some comments on this survey see Jenifer Hart, 'Some Reflections on the Report of the Royal Commission on the Police', *Public Law* (1963) 283.

In the majority recommendations for dealing with complaints the local authorities were given an odd task. They were told to 'satisfy themselves' that complaints were properly dealt with, but it was added that they would have 'no power to intervene in a particular case'. It remained vague whether requests for reports might relate to particular instances. And suppose the authority were not satisfied? How were they supposed to satisfy themselves?

THE CENTRAL AUTHORITY

Under the Commission's scheme local authorities as public relations officers and paymasters were presumably intended to act in any substantive matter only through the Home Secretary. But in defining the exact sphere of authority which should pass to the Home Office the Report is imprecise and inconsistent. What, consistently with the argument of the earlier chapters, *ought* to have been transferred was responsibility in some degree for what were there called 'police policies' raising general questions of policing in its operational sense. But this it turned out was not the Commission's recommendation after all, since the Secretary of State's duties under the proposed régime were not to extend 'beyond a general duty to see that the police operate efficiently'. It was to be only a responsibility for 'an efficient organization both central and local'. There was, it was suggested, 'a fundamental distinction' between this and the *'responsibility of the police themselves,* which is neither central nor local, for the enforcement of the law' (para. 230). But what had become of those aspects of enforcement which the Commission earlier argued ought *not* to be the sole responsibility of the police themselves? The Home Secretary was not clearly said to have the responsibility of challenge in this field. He was not to be in control of policy in the sense in which he is in control of policy and operations in the metropolitan area. Yet any responsibility which the local authority might have had would have been removed from it under the Commission's scheme.

The Report emphasized that the Secretary of State could not be responsible for 'the acts of individual policemen or for the day-to-day enforcement of the law'. So there was not to be 'challenge' in the House of Commons sense for provincial police operations either centrally or locally. In the House of Commons it is often precisely aberrations or alleged aberrations in day-to-day enforcement matters and acts of individual policemen which raise legitimate questions of public interest. Constitutionally the House of Commons could make use of the Home Secretary's responsibility for the metropolitan police by asking him to give orders in either general or particular cases – though they could not without passing a statute ask him to give illegal orders in contravention of the existing law. No such relationship as this was proposed between the Home Secretary and the provincial police. Indeed the Secretaries of State were to have no powers of direction, even apparently within the sphere of efficiency.

In view of the importance which the Commissioners attached to their transfer of statutory responsibility for efficiency to the Home Secretary it is surprising that they should have had nothing whatsoever to say about parliamentary responsibility under the Willink plan. What sorts of questions should be allowable about police activity outside London? Were the Speaker and Chairman of Committees to go on applying the old restrictive rulings or was it desirable that they should follow the sorts of precedents set by questions to Ministers on nationalized industries? All this was, of course, in the end a matter for the House of Commons and Parliament itself. But then, so was everything else about which the Commission was making recommendations. On so central a matter one might have expected the Commissioners to have stated an opinion; but they left the topic undebated.

7 The Police Act, 1964

THE REPORT OF THE ROYAL COMMISSION WAS DEBATED IN THE House of Commons on 9 May 1963. The only member of the House who had served on the Commission throughout its investigations, Mr Leslie Hale, made his usual lively incursion with some informative glimpses of the Commission's proceedings. They had met, he said, 'not only chiefs of police in their dotage, but several who were in their ripe anecdotage'.

> We went to one borough, a very important one, where we found that the former chief constable had been absent from duty almost continuously for years. Every time the pigeon shooting season began on the Riviera he gave himself long sick leave and the corporation had never seen the report of the inspector of constabulary . . . We said, 'What about it?' Members of the corporation said, 'We wanted it, but think what would happen if we reported the matter to the Home Office. They would send him back.'

The Commission had tried hard, he said, to reach unanimity:

> I recall briefly a famous story by O. Henry about the young lady who was living alone, exposed to the temptations of a great city, eating biscuits and drinking cold milk and watched by a picture of Lord Kitchener over the bed . . . I became conscious of a picture looking down on me. It had a touch of Machiavelli and a touch of the Mona Lisa as described by Walter Pater . . . Underneath it was the simple legend, 'R.A.B.' . . . while that picture looked down it struck me that we had better have a unanimous report. It struck others of us too and we tried very hard.[1]

[1] 677 H.C. Deb. 5s. cols. 128–30.

Mr Butler's successor at the Home Office, Mr Henry Brooke, opened the debate for the Government. In introducing the Bill he thanked the Chairman and members of the Commission and said that he looked on their report as opening a new chapter in the long and famous history of the police. This sentiment was not universally shared. Dr A. L. Goodhart, the author of the minority recommendation, was recorded by *The Times* as suggesting that the Home Secretary had 'spoken of the report in glowing terms and then killed it stone dead'. This was the natural reaction of those who saw the essence of the Report in its proposals for increasing the amount of central control exercised over the police. Commenting on 17 May, the *Police Review* thought that 'the most important thing to emerge from the House of Commons debate . . . is that the Home Secretary does not intend to accept the key recommendation . . . that legal responsibility for the efficient policing of an area should be transferred from police authorities to Secretaries of State and that the Secretaries of State should be made statutorily responsible for the efficiency of the police'. It is doubtful whether most people have been as clear in their minds as Mr Brooke about the difference between the rejected concept of having a statutory responsibility for the efficiency of the police and the statutory duty (which the Home Secretary was willing to accept) of exercising his powers in such a way as appeared to him best calculated to promote the efficiency of the police. Mr Brooke's words in the debate were: 'I am not disposed to accept the Commission's recommendation that I should assume a general statutory responsibility for the efficiency of the police. A Minister ought not to have responsibility without power.'[1] What he proposed to do was to take powers to call for reports from chief constables, to effect the retirement of chief constables and to ensure that adequate arrangements were made for securing co-operation between, and where necessary amalgamation of, forces. Given the existence of these powers, the correlative responsibility seems one that is not easy to distinguish from a statutory responsibility for efficiency, especially when added to the powers to make regulations, to inspect and if necessary to withhold the police grant.

[1] 677 H.C. Deb. 5s. col. 689.

Many, indeed, have thought that the Home Secretary has always had, jointly with local police authorities, a statutory responsibility for efficiency. The Home Secretary's view seemed to be based upon the supposition that the power which should accompany responsibility could only be of one kind, namely to control and give orders rather than to inspect, finance or secure reports. But the latter kinds of power at least carry with them some statutory and parliamentary responsibility. There seems in fact to be no matter of efficiency upon which the Secretary of State could not ask for a report, or be asked in turn by a member why he had not done so. On this occasion, however, he suggested that the right to call for reports would enable him to give Parliament information about police matters outside the metropolis – 'though not to answer for matters which do not engage my statutory responsibility'.[1] It was entirely unclear what matters the Home Secretary believed would fail to engage his responsibility. The extent to which detailed parliamentary questioning was to be possible remained, therefore, unclarified.

On the nationalization issue the Government had already made up its mind and the decision had been announced by Mr R. A. Butler in June of the previous year.[2] The Government agreed, Mr Brooke went on, that the local basis of police organization should be preserved. Some action had already been taken in line with the Commission's recommendations. A Chief Inspector of Constabulary had been appointed, the number of inspectors had been increased to seven and a police research and planning branch was being set up in the Home Office.[3] A circular had been sent to local authorities and chief constables commending to them nineteen of the Commission's minor administrative recommendations.[4]

[1] 677 H.C. Deb. 5s. col. 688.

[2] Announcing the decision to the Annual Joint Conference of Chief Police Officers and Police Authorities Mr Butler said 'I am quite convinced that it would be wrong for one man or one government to be in charge directly of the whole police of this country. Our constitution is based on checks and balances. This has kept our liberty through the generations.' The Times, 27 June 1962.

[3] More details have since been given in Cmnd. 2296 The War Against Crime in England and Wales 1959–1964, pp. 4ff.

[4] The Commission's recommendation of quicker promotion has been partially implemented by the Police (Promotion) (Amendment) Regulations, 1964, which

86

As to the functions of the local police authority the Home Secretary saw no reason for any radical change. It was not clear whether he believed that the Royal Commission had recommended any radical change, but the statement of police authority function which he went on to mention (to maintain and equip an adequate force; to appoint a chief constable and to share with the Home Secretary in determining the establishment of the force) seemed to owe a good deal to the somewhat diminished definition of status proposed for the local authorities by the Commission. Was it merely an accident that any mention of responsibility for efficient policing was omitted from the Home Secretary's formulation? Perhaps so, since he proposed to add to the police authorities' functions the power to require a chief constable to retire in the interests of efficiency,[1] subject to the Secretary of State's agreement, and the power to call for reports from chief constables. The Secretary of State himself would also have power to get a chief constable retired 'on the ground of efficiency'. (Mr Charles Pannell here interjected that 'inefficiency' would be a more appropriate ground and Mr Brooke, after some thought, conceded the point.)

The suggestions that watch committees should cease to exercise their statutory power, contained in the nineteenth-century statutes, of summary dismissal of police officers, and also that powers of appointment, promotion and discipline should be transferred to borough chief constables, were proposals with which the Government was disposed to agree. The Royal Commission's suggestion that both borough and county police authorities should include magistrates as one-third of the committee's membership was also to be implemented. As to the size of forces the Government did not propose to appoint the review body which the Royal Commission had in mind, but to await the conclusions of the local government commissions for England and Wales and then to ask the Chief Inspector of Constabulary and his colleagues to advise on possible

provide that the normal qualifying service for promotion to sergeant shall be four years (instead of five) and that the promotion examination may be taken in three instead of four years.

[1] It may be noted that power to secure retirement 'in the general interests of efficiency' could already be exercised under the Police Pensions Regulations, 1955.

87

amalgamations which would be carried out by consultation between the Secretary of State and local police authorities. There was no intention to apply strict arithmetical criteria of the kind mentioned by the Royal Commission.

The proposals outlined by the Home Secretary were published in draft form in November 1963 and the Police Bill received its second reading in the Commons on 26 November. Introducing it the Home Secretary claimed that in some respects the Government had gone further than the Royal Commission. The Bill went far, for example, in repealing old law. More than twenty Acts were repealed outright and many more partially repealed. In consequence the new measure was 'a succinct and comprehensive statement of the fundamental law relating to police organization'.[1]

The Home Secretary's claim may certainly be accepted. The Bill was in fact both comprehensive and succinct. But it is possible to obtain succinctness without removing ambiguity and on some of the fundamental points of the scheme obscurity remained. Two such points were the implications of the new powers to call for reports given to police authorities and the nature of the Home Secretary's parliamentary responsibility, already debated somewhat inconclusively in the debate of the previous May.

On the latter point, however, some interesting exchanges took place during the course of the Home Secretary's second reading speech. He was now, he said, to have more responsibility for the police and must therefore be 'answerable to Parliament for police affairs to a greater extent than hitherto'. When the Bill was on the statute book it would be possible for Members to put down more questions about police matters outside London. Members would be able to ask questions on matters within the Home Secretary's responsibility – 'But that does not mean that they will be able to ask any questions they like.' That would depend on the interpretation of the Table and of the Speaker.[2] Several members wanted to explore this point.

[1] 685 H.C. Deb. 5s. col. 82.
[2] 685 H.C. Debs. 5s. col. 86. It will obviously also depend upon the view of his responsibility taken by the Home Secretary.

SIR KENNETH THOMPSON . . . As I understand it, hon. Members would be in order, subject to the direction of the Chair, in putting down Questions, for example about the use by a chief constable of mounted police to restore order in the event of trouble but that it would not be in order for members of the watch committee or police authority concerned to question their own chief constable about the same thing.

MR BROOKE My hon. Friend has it wrong. Unquestionably the police authority could ask for a report from the chief constable on that and could discuss the report with me.

SIR K. THOMPSON But he could refuse to give it.

MR BROOKE If he did the matter would be settled in the end by the Home Secretary. But in a case like that I can see no reason why the chief constable should not supply a report on request on a matter like that.

As I understand it, however, it will be for the Home Secretary to decide these matters . . . and he will be open to question, for example whether he will call for a report from the chief constable, whether he will insist that an inquiry shall be made by a senior officer of another force and so forth.

MR A. J. IRVINE Would not the chief constable be entitled to submit to the right hon. Gentleman that a report given to him should not be given also to the local police authority?

MR BROOKE He would be entitled to make that submission but he would be overruled by me if I were Home Secretary.   ·

Mr Brooke went on to say that a police authority would have 'every right to discuss with its chief constable *how the men and equipment with which it has provided him can be most effectively used in conducting police operations* though they would not be able to issue instructions.'[1] If, he went on, the hon. Member found difficult the concept of a person being accountable to a body of people who, nevertheless, could not give him orders, there was 'something of a parallel in the relationship of all of us with our constituents. We are accountable to them and they can dismiss us but they cannot give us orders.' The point was an ingenious one but, if valid, it provided a petard apt to hoist the Home Secretary from the position which he had adopted in arguing that the police could not be regarded as generally accountable to him in matters of efficiency. His only reason for

[1] *Ibid.*, col. 87 (italics added).

maintaining that proposition had been that the Home Secretary's powers of supervision and inquiry did not include a power to instruct or control and there could be no 'responsibility without power'. Yet the suggestion here was that no difficulty at all existed in the notion of an accountability to a body not in a position to instruct or control. In almost the next breath, however, Mr Brooke was insisting once more that the Bill did not go so far as to make him legally responsible for the efficiency of the police. What the Bill did was to place upon the Home Secretary a statutory duty to exercise his powers so as to promote the efficiency of the police. It would seem that for the proper exercise of that statutory duty the Home Secretary is responsible to the House of Commons. But he cannot be described as 'responsible for the efficiency of the police'. Mr Gladstone would have been pleased with the distinction.

Parliamentary accountability was the subject of a number of other interventions in the debate. Mr G. R. Howard wanted to know whether Members would be able to ask questions on detailed matters as well as on general policy. 'We do not,' he said, 'want to be fobbed off by being told that the question raised is a matter of detailed administration and not one of general policy for the Home Secretary, because in police matters it is the specific case which can raise important issues of liberty.'[1] The Home Secretary had not, in fact, led Members to expect any such rebuff. He had, it is true, said that they would not be able to ask any question they liked, but his exchange with Sir Kenneth Thompson had implied that at least some particular matters affecting police activities would be matters which it would be proper to question in the House. The example about the use of mounted police on a particular occasion had been put forward as an instance of something upon which the local authority could call for a report and as something which they could discuss with the Home Secretary. If they could do that, it would seem possible for M.P.s to ask the Home Secretary about the result of his conversations. They could also presumably found a question upon a request to the Home Secretary to seek a report upon an individual incident. Mr Charles Royle, however, wanted a more

[1] Col. 106.

precise assurance. The Home Secretary, he suggested, had said that he would be open to question as to whether he would call for a report or set up an inquiry into a local matter but he had not specifically said that Members could 'rise in the House and say, I have an accusation here from one of my constituents. What is the answer to it?' That was the sort of accountability, Mr Royle suggested, for which they had been fighting year after year. Other members, similarly, wanted assurances that every report, both those asked for by local police authorities and those asked for by the Secretary of State, would be subject to question in the House.

Mr Arthur Holt saw some difficulties in the questioning of detailed matters. If Members were to be able to put detailed questions this would involve the Home Secretary's using his powers of inquiry not as a last resort but as a matter of everyday routine and his actively and frequently receiving reports from chief constables about local incidents. If the Home Secretary was prepared for this and to answer questions such as 'What happened when a policeman was involved in a scuffle outside the Nag's Head in Salford last Saturday night', it would make a great difference to the structure and working of the police service, and they were entitled to a clear answer on this point. If, he continued, the House became a place where the most searching questions were continuously asked and answered about police forces, it could not but bring about a diminution in the standing and position of the local police authorities. The Home Secretary had said that he was taking further powers for himself but not diminishing the powers of the local authority. That was not mathematically possible. If there were two masters and the power of one was increased the power of the other must be diminished.[1] Mr Holt's analogy was in some degree imperfect. It implied the overlooking of a third mathematical possibility, namely that both the central and the local authority might have increased their powers equally at the expense of the police. What the Joint Under-Secretary of State Mr C. M. Woodhouse in fact claimed in replying to the debate was that some power had at least been taken from the chief constables by the Secretary of State. As to questions

[1] At cols. 178-9.

in the House, they would have to proceed, he thought, by a process of trial and error. Subject to considerations of security and the public interest, however, he could assure the House that the Home Secretary would certainly give to it the information obtained by way of reports from chief constables. Nevertheless the House could not expect 'to interfere in every detail'. Leaving aside the question whether the possibility of asking for and getting information may be described as 'interference', it remained uncertain whether Mr Woodhouse's suggestion was that the Minister would not be inclined to answer certain types of detailed question or that such questions would be out of order as falling outside his responsibility.

As to the matters on which local police authorities might properly call for reports, Mr Woodhouse suggested that they would include the state of crime, the extent of police protection in a particular district, how the force was disposed between crime and traffic and other duties, and particular incidents which might have given rise to complaints. To sum up, he thought the matter of responsibility could be stated as follows: 'The police authority will be responsible for providing an efficient instrument and *supervising its use*. The chief constable will be responsible for using that instrument efficiently.'[1]

This definition of the function of a local police authority is at least wider than that which has sometimes been allotted to it or than was implied by the recommendations of the Royal Commission. The concern for efficiency goes further on this view than financing, equipping and maintaining the force, or than the parliamentary ruling that efficiency relates to 'whether the men are properly drilled, properly trained and properly clothed'.[2] But it leaves open the question of the extent of 'supervision' of the instrument provided.

Though both the central authority and the local police authority have the duty of supervising and promoting efficient policing there remains a certain asymmetry between the two sets of powers. There seems no restriction as to the matters which the Home Secretary may inquire into by way of report in the exercise of his promotion of efficiency. As was said when the Police Bill was in committee, 'recognition that the scope of the Secretary of State's legitimate in-

---

[1] Col. 203 (italics added).   [2] See above, p. 51.

terest coincided with that of the police authority's . . . would be unacceptable to the Government. The Bill imposes no limit and is intended to impose no limit on the matters on which the Secretary of State can call for reports.'[1] Thus the legislation envisages that the obtaining of reports on at least some matters is not required by the local police authority for the proper discharge of its supervisory function since chief constables may decline to furnish a report on this ground.[2] If there are such matters they ought in theory to be as much outside the purview of the Home Secretary as of the police authority. This indeed would be the logic of the view propounded by the Royal Commission – that the responsibility of the police themselves for the enforcement of the law is 'neither central nor local'.[3] There seems a tendency to accept this principle when denying powers to police authorities and to deny it when giving powers to the Secretary of State.

From the speeches made on the second reading and in committee the Home Office's expressed intentions in drafting the Police Bill could be set out as provisional answers to the following series of questions about police authority powers:

1. May they ask for information or reports on the administration, training and equipment of the force? Answer: Yes.
2. May they issue instructions as to administrative matters in this sense. Answer: Yes, at least as to some such matters.
3. May they ask for general information or reports on police operations and disposition of forces? Answer: Yes, subject to the chief constable's right of refusal.
4. May they issue instructions as to general policies involved in police operations and disposition of forces? Answer: No.
5. May they ask for information or reports on particular incidents or enforcement measures? Answer: Yes, subject to the chief constable's right of refusal.
6. May they issue instructions as to particular enforcement measures or arising out of particular incidents? Answer: No.
7. May they ask for information or reports on the institution or withdrawal

[1] Standing Committee D, 23 January 1964, col. 421 (Mr Woodhouse).
[2] Section 12(3) of the Act (see below).
[3] Royal Commission Report, para. 230.

of either particular classes of prosecutions or of individual prosecutions? Answer: Uncertain.

It may still be questioned, however, whether these answers are the right ones and whether the corresponding principles have been unambiguously written into the Police Act.

PROVISIONS OF THE 1964 ACT

The Act itself is a thoroughgoing codification of existing police legislation in England and Wales and contains amendments to the Police (Scotland) Act of 1956. Part 1 deals with the organization of police forces, Part 2 with central supervision and facilities regulated by the Home Secretary, Part 3 with police representative institutions and Part 4 with miscellaneous matters including remedies and complaints against the police and several criminal offences affecting constables, such as assault, obstruction and impersonation.

Composition of Police Authorities (s. 2). Section 2 of the Act carries out the recommendation of the Royal Commission that for both counties and county boroughs the police authority should be a committee of the council and that in each case a third of the members should be magistrates. County police authorities are to be known as 'police committees' and borough authorities 'watch committees'. They are to consist of such number of persons as the county or borough council may determine and the magistrates are to be appointed in the counties by quarter sessions and in the boroughs by the borough magistrates.

This provision was a contentious one at each stage of the Bill's progress. In opposing amendments at the Committee stage the Government argued that police authorities would be greatly assisted by the inclusion of a proportion of justices; that the county councils desired to retain magistrates among their membership and that the only way to assimilate the county and borough systems was to include magistrates also on watch committees. They did not believe that these arguments were outweighed by the possible dilution of the democratically elected element or by the possibility of a confusing of executive and judicial functions. The democratic element in the counties was actually being strengthened (since half of the

94

county standing joint committees had hitherto been magistrates as against the proposed third) and the county system which had worked well, it was said, ought not to be abolished on any 'doctrinaire' ground. Opposition members were inclined to believe that doctrinaire grounds had had something to do with the composition of the county committees in the first place. It had been Tory fright, in 1888, said Mr Chuter Ede, which after the extension of the county franchise had led to the inclusion of magistrates on police authorities in the counties, so as to preserve the traditional power of the landed classes. They were afraid that the radical spirit of Joseph Arch might dominate the county councils.[1] The county system, another member thought, was 'an overspill of feudalism'.

Mr O'Malley, also opposing the clause as it stood, suggested that magistrates were not necessarily independent in view of their mode of selection. They were not 'people with no political bias who are not concerned with the large political issues of the day, who have no social life and no social circles and who come down from Olympian heights to guide and help'.[2] The Under-Secretary of State for his part denied that the inclusion of magistrates was proposed on account of any suspicion of political bias on the part of elected members. He agreed with Aristotle that Man was a political animal. They were not suggesting that politics was a dirty game which needed Olympian intervention. Indeed 'the Olympians were an unsavoury lot and there was nothing very creditable about any of their interventions in human affairs'.[3]

The disclaimer of an obvious motive for the insistence on the inclusion of magistrates puts an odd air on the Government's argument. If the reasons are merely that some technical advantages in the working of police authorities are to be obtained by the inclusion of people familiar with the police and police problems they do not seem solid enough on any reasonable calculation to outweigh the arguments which may be brought against the use of magistrates as members of the police authority. Elsewhere, and in particular in the magistrates' courts themselves, efforts have been made to dissociate

---

[1] Police Bill, Standing Committee D, 3 December 1963, col. 25.
[2] *Ibid.*, col. 38.   [3] *Ibid.*, cols. 64–5.

the police and the judiciary. Arguments of principle against the scheme were developed before the Royal Commission by a wide body of opinion, including the Law Society, the Bow Group and the Inns of Court Conservative and Unionist Society. The rejection of these arguments as 'doctrinaire' only makes tactical sense if done for some major advantage. The belief in some need for a counter-balance to the possibility of political bias in the elected membership of borough watch committees was not, perhaps, one which the Government could have comfortably deployed in the Commons but in resisting the amendments and resting so strongly on the Royal Commission's recommendation at this particular point they may well have been a little less than frank.

Functions of Police Authorities and Chief Constables (ss. 4, 5, 12, 48). Section 4 defines the duty of a police authority as being 'to secure the maintenance of an adequate and efficient police force for the area'. The use of the word 'adequate' does not, it would seem from the assurances given in the House of Commons, indicate any intention to confine watch committees and police committees to matters of establishment and provisioning. At the same time it is equally clear that Ministers in 1964 took the view that in any operational matter a police authority should have no power to instruct a chief constable. Nevertheless this thesis has not been reflected in any clear statutory enactment, and it can be argued that the law on this point remains unclear. In so far as ministerial views have been implemented they can perhaps be seen in the provision in section 5 that 'The police force . . . shall be under the direction and control of the chief constable' and in the facilities provided for the chief constable to invoke the arbitration of the Secretary of State in relation to the police authority's exercise of its powers under the Act. The explicit powers conferred on a police authority are to appoint the chief constable, to secure his retirement (subject to the Secretary of State's approval) if they think it necessary 'in the interests of efficiency' and to receive or require reports from the chief constable. The chief constable is to submit annually a general report in writing 'on the policing' of the area. In addition he is, whenever so required, to submit to the authority a report in writing 'on such matters as may be specified in the requirement, being matters connected with the policing of the area'. There seems in this provision a clear enough assumption that any matter which the authority believes to be a matter of policing is a proper matter for it at least to inquire into. Yet on the other hand, there is in the following clause the contrary assumption, already noted, that some matters are not matters which the police authority may even seek information upon. Section 12 provides that if it appears to the chief constable that any particular request for a report relates to matters which ought not to be disclosed in the public interest or to information 'not needed for the discharge of the functions of the police authority' he may decline to report and refer the requirement to the Secretary of State. The local authority representations to the Home Office were to the effect that it ought not to be for a chief constable to decide whether or not information is needed for the discharge of the police authority's functions. However, it will in effect be the Home Secretary who is the arbiter. It is not clear what general types of information will be thought by the Home Secretary to be 'not required' by police authorities, or on what principles chief constables are expected to act in refusing to comply with requests to report. Many chief constables may perforce have had to form their own views in the past as to the ambit of their police authority's powers. Some may have taken narrower views than others. But that was before the legislature had clearly conferred a general right to inquire into what it has described as 'matters concerned with the policing of the area', and that is a fairly comprehensive description under which police authorities might reasonably expect to reap at least some benefits of earlier doubts about the limits of their functions.

What of the power to issue instructions? Local police authorities could and did claim before the passing of the Act that there was nothing in the law to prevent a police authority from issuing instructions to a chief constable on some matters of general policy affecting law-enforcement operations. Despite the categorical views expressed by Ministers in opposition to this claim, it is suggested that the Act itself does not put the issue beyond question. It provides that a police force shall be under the direction and control of the chief constable, but it could be argued that these words merely describe the existing situation. Chief constables have always exercised the immediate direction and control of their forces. The question whether they themselves are to any extent under the general control of the police authority is another matter. The Act does not use any such phrase as 'exclusive control of the chief constable'. It does not in terms enact anything at all about the hierarchical relationship between the chief constable himself and the police authority responsible (in the Home Office's phrase) for 'supervising the use' of the instrument which the chief constable wields. No doubt the Home Secretary will be able to enforce his own view of the situation, since he can always be appealed to against any sanctions which a police authority can bring to bear. But the Police Act itself has not decisively enacted into law the conclusions which were drawn by some from *Fisher v. Oldham Corporation*. Indeed it has helped to demonstrate the original irrelevance of that decision to the more general implications inferred from it. For the doctrine that chief constables were not subject to control in law enforcement matters rested squarely upon the proposition that they were constables at common law; and the notion that constables at common law exercised independent powers rested in turn upon the doctrine that they were not in a master and servant relationship with anyone for purposes of civil liability.[1] That particular rule is now abolished and constables are in effect placed in a master and servant relationship with chief constables by s. 48 of the Police Act.[2] The individual constable's 'responsibility to the law' for the exercise of his common law powers presumably remains compatible with this arrangement and means as much or as little as it did before the Act.

---

[1] See above, Chap. 3.

[2] Rather than with the police authority as recommended by the Royal Commission. The section provides that 'The chief officer of police for any police area shall be liable in respect of torts committed by constables under his direction and control in the performance or purported performance of their functions in like manner as a master is liable in respect of torts committed by his servants in the course of their employment and accordingly shall in respect of any such tort be treated for all purposes as a joint tortfeasor.'

Any damages awarded against a chief officer in proceedings brought against him under the Act are to be paid out of the police fund, though any sum needed to meet any settlement of a claim which is agreed by the chief constable must be approved by the police authority. The police authority, in such cases and to such extent as they think fit, may pay any damages or costs awarded against any individual constable of the force maintained by them.

Two additional powers of some importance are conferred on chief constables. S. 33 gives effect to the Royal Commission's recommendation that borough chief constables rather than the watch committee should be the disciplinary authority in relation to subordinate ranks in the force (though the police authority remains the disciplinary authority in relation to chief constables and deputy or assistant chief constables). S. 13 provides that chief constables can, with the approval of the police authority, make arrangements for the joint discharge of functions between two or more police forces if it appears to them that any such functions can be more efficiently discharged by such collaboration. Police authorities for any two or more areas may also submit to the Secretary of State proposals for the amalgamation of the areas for police purposes.

Duties of the Secretary of State (ss. 21, 28–42). For the purpose of securing the amalgamation of areas the Home Secretary may act on his own initiative[1] and make such a scheme where it appears to him expedient in the interests of efficiency and where no scheme satisfactory to him has been submitted. His general duty under the Act is to use his powers 'in such manner and to such extent as appears to him to be best calculated to promote the efficiency of the police'. To this end he may require a police authority to use their power to call for the retirement of a chief constable in the interests of efficiency (first giving any such chief constable the opportunity to make representations to him). Like the local police authority, the Secretary of State may require a chief constable to submit a report on any matter connected with the policing of the area, and chief constables are also

[1] The Home Secretary's first proposals under the Act were for an amalgamation of the Luton force with Bedfordshire and the Northampton force with Northamptonshire.

required to provide the Home Secretary with a copy of the annual report made to the police authority. There does not seem to be complete reciprocity, however, between the Home Secretary and the police authority in the matter of reports. There is the Home Secretary's assurance[1] that he would be reluctant to allow a report asked for by the police authority to be made to him without being shown to the authority. On the other hand it was said in Committee that the Government could not undertake that in all cases the local authority would have a copy of a report asked for by the Home Secretary. Possible examples are reports calling for certain kinds of information needed to answer parliamentary questions,[2] or other allegations made by Members of Parliament about police powers which might necessitate inquiries by the Secretary of State; and security matters. In the first two cases it is understandable that the Home Secretary might feel unable to make the contents of a report known to the local authority before they had been given to Parliament or used to answer the relevant question. But this would not in itself be a reason for withholding the report afterwards. There does not seem in general any very good reason why (aside from matters affecting national security) anything which is appropriate for report to the Secretary of State should be inappropriate material for the information of a police authority if it is properly to perform its supervisory function.

The Secretary of State is given, by s. 32, a formal power of inquiry. He may cause such inquiry to be made by any person appointed by him and the inquiry is expressed as being into 'any matter connected with the policing of any area'. The powers of summoning and examining witnesses conferred by s. 290 of the Local Government Act, 1933, are to apply to any such local inquiry.

[1] See above, p. 89.
[2] This example is perhaps an uncertain one since the remarks made about parliamentary questions by Ministers during the debates on the Bill were not at all clear. In Committee the Joint Under-Secretary of State said 'it is not possible to give a complete undertaking that in all such cases the local authority would either have a copy of the report or be informed of the matters under report. This would not be so for instance in the case of a report calling for information for answer to a parliamentary question.' (Standing Committee D, 23 January 1964, col. 421.)

The inspectors of constabulary whose duty is to report to the Secretary of State on efficiency may also under s. 38 be required by him to carry out such other duties for the purpose of furthering efficiency as he may from time to time direct. This somewhat vague provision seems intended to give the inspectorate specific authority actively to promote and recommend to the various forces measures of collaboration and to secure the adoption of the fruits of research on police methods conducted by the Home Office or elsewhere.

A further incident of collaboration between forces appears in s. 19 of the Act by which a restriction on the jurisdiction of constables has been removed, and a constable in any force is to have 'all the powers and privileges of a constable throughout England and Wales'.

Investigation of Complaints (ss. 49–50). S. 49 places a statutory obligation on chief constables to record 'forthwith' and to investigate any complaint from a member of the public against a member of the force (unless the allegation relates to an offence with which the member of the police force has already been charged). In causing the complaint to be investigated the chief constable may, and if the Home Secretary so directs must, request the chief constable of some other police area to carry out the investigation. The report of an investigation under this section is to be sent to the Director of Public Prosecutions unless the chief constable is satisfied from the report that no criminal offence has been committed. 'An investigation under this section' presumably is not confined to the more formal reports made by an external investigating officer but includes the investigations made by the chief constable himself. The provision is plainly designed to remove from a chief constable the burden of deciding whether or not to prosecute a member of his own force.

Opposition amendments were put down to provide for a form of complaints review by a body not drawn from the police service but were resisted by the Government. The Home Secretary's view was that 'to contemplate bringing an entirely outside person or functionary, whether a commissioner of rights or an ombudsman or whatever he may be called, to investigate any complaint that a member of the public however irresponsible may see fit to make against the police is to run serious risks with the morale of the service'.[1] It was not the time, he added later, 'to introduce reforms which the police might well distrust and which might . . . lead some of them to pull their punches'.[2]

It would seem that investigations for which outside officers are called in will not be formal hearings in which there is a right of appearance and cross-examination by the complainant. Complainants will be witnesses rather than parties and statements will be taken from them by the investigating officer as from other witnesses. This, it was stated in the House, would formally be the position also at a disciplinary hearing under the police discipline regulations, but at such hearings complainants will be allowed to be present and to put questions through the presiding officer.[3] At the local inquiries appointed by the Secretary of State under s.32 the person appointed by the Minister to hold the inquiry will apparently decide the form of procedure to be used.

Under s. 50 of the Act both the local police authority and the inspectors of constabulary are given a duty to keep themselves informed as to the manner in which complaints are dealt with by the chief constable. No procedure is laid down in the Act to facilitate the carrying out of this duty, but it would seem that the authority's power to ask for reports could reasonably be used to secure information about the handling of complaints.[4]

Questions to Local Police Authorities. S. 11 which was inserted at the Committee stage may prove to be one of the most significant provisions in the Act. It provides that

Arrangements shall be made (whether by standing orders or otherwise) for enabling questions on the discharge of the functions of the police

[1] 685 H.C. Deb. 5s. col. 94.

[2] Standing Committee D, 13 February 1964, cols. 708–9. For the committee debate on complaints procedure, see *ibid.*, 11–13 February, cols. 639–729.

[3] 685 H.C. Deb. 5s. col. 208.

[4] The complaints themselves are to be recorded in a book at divisional headquarters which should be open to inspection by the police authority. (*Home Office Circular* 103/63.)

authority for any county, county borough or combined area to be put in the course of the proceedings of the council for that county or county borough or, as the case may be, of a constituent council, by members of that council for answer by a member thereof who is also a member of the police authority and is nominated by that authority for that purpose.

The extent to which this will involve innovations in local authority procedure is unclear. It is a common practice for members of councils to be able to ask questions on the report of committees including the watch committee but it may not be the custom to permit supplementaries or further probing of the answers in the way that is usual when Ministers are questioned in the House of Commons. Some Members were unhappy about this when the clause was debated. The putting of a simple question and the receiving of a simple answer did not, they thought, cover what they had in mind and the clause should, it was argued, have been more explicit. There was also – and is – some uncertainty about the type of questioning which should be permitted. The Home Secretary, in introducing the clause, suggested that questions would now be put – 'but not in such a way as to enable the council to exercise some sort of control, apart from financial control over the police authority'.[1] This might suggest that the scope of questioning should be restricted to the financial sphere. But the Act itself states clearly enough that the questions may be directed to the 'discharge of the functions of the police authority'. The view expressed about control seemed confused. Questions do not in themselves, in any event, exercise a control. But if their purpose is not indirectly at least to influence and control those who are questioned about their functions what is their purpose? The Royal Commission when it recommended that steps should be taken to provide machinery for local questioning on police matters was not thinking merely of the satisfaction of councillors' idle curiosity about police work. It would seem obviously to be the case that questions are a form of at least indirect control and that they may range over non-financial matters. Members of Parliament in debating this provision clearly had a wide field in

[1] Standing Committee D, 20 February 1964, col. 815.

mind. They were anxious to know whether questions could be asked 'on discipline, about complaints and about the numerous matters which arise in the administration of the police and which never see the light of day in most local authorities in the form of either minutes or publicity?'[1] The answer to all such inquiries comes back to the question: what is the ambit of the watch committee's powers? Since it was conceded in the debates on the Police Bill that these powers extended to the supervision of police operations at least in the sense that reports could be called for on such matters as the state of crime, the disposition of the force and particular incidents giving rise to complaints, a useful rule of thumb would seem to be that questions should be in order in the council chamber on any matter which it would be proper for the watch committee or police committee to make the subject of a request for report from the chief constable. Since reports may, as stated in section 12, be required on any matter 'connected with the policing of the area', the scope for questioning ought in principle to be wide. But since the watch committee's power to secure reports is restricted by the chief constable's right of refusal, will presiding officers and town clerks, as well as chief constables, feel called upon to decide that some questions are out of order as touching information relating to the policing of the area but 'not needed for the discharge of the functions of the police authority'? How is a mayor, chairman or council clerk to decide this? The better course would seem to be to place as few restrictions as possible on the ambit of questioning and leave the chairman of the police authority or whoever is nominated by it to decline to answer or to take the suggested action. In many cases it would seem likely that the chairman (like a minister in relation to some affairs of public corporations) will only be able to say that he will ask for information or for a report from the chief constable – which he may prove unable to get. It will be interesting to see, however, what use council members make of their opportunities.

[1] Standing Committee D, 20 February 1964, col. 827.

8 Police Accountability: Some Conclusions

SINCE THE DRAFTING OF THE NEW LEGISLATION, THE PRO-
priety of police behaviour has been in question on a number of
occasions. In a number of cases formal inquiries were set on foot by
the Home Secretary. The first resulted from the dismissal in 1963 of
two Sheffield detectives who had pleaded guilty and had been fined
for serious assaults on prisoners. It was conducted by Mr Graham
Russell Swanwick, Q.C., and Commander W. J. A. Willis, an
inspector of constabulary, and took place as an appeal hearing by
the dismissed men under the Police Appeals Acts, 1927. The inquiry
ranged over a wide field, since among the grounds of appeal were
allegations that the assaults had been committed on the instructions
and under the supervision of senior officers and that the guilt of
other officers had been hushed up. The tribunal found that the
appellants had been guilty of 'brutal and sustained assaults with
weapons of the nature of a truncheon and a short flexible piece of
gut-like material ... for the purpose of inducing confessions of
crime'.[1] They also found that the detectives in question had been under
pressure to obtain results, that violence had been encouraged before-
hand and witnessed with approval by senior officers and that a senior
officer had concocted and instigated them to put forward a false story
in mitigation before the Justices. The chief constable's attitude, the
report added, had been influenced partly by a reluctance to believe
that men under his command could be guilty of infamous conduct
and partly by a view that the local press were hostile to the police, so
that it was undesirable to attract more publicity than was necessary.

---

[1] *Sheffield Police Inquiry*, Cmnd. 2176 (1963), p. 29.

The Police Act does something to remedy the predicament of a chief constable who has in future to make decisions to prosecute or refrain from prosecuting members of his force, since he will be under an obligation to consult the Director of Public Prosecutions whenever in doubt about the institution of proceedings.

The suspicion of violence led to a second independent inquiry in December of the same year. The inquiry on this occasion was into the action of the metropolitan police in relation to the case of Mr Herman Woolf[1] and was carried out by Mr Norman Skelhorn, Q.C. (later appointed as Solicitor-General). Mr Woolf was knocked down by a car in November 1962, and after examination in hospital was handed over to the police and charged with being in possession of drugs. His injuries were then found to be more serious than had been thought and he was removed once more into hospital where he died. The injured man's wife was not informed that he was in police custody between the time of his arrest on 10 November and the time of his death on the 23rd. The report of the inquiry concluded that though there had been a failure of the missing persons procedure and an improper search of the prisoner's premises, he had not been subjected to any violence or maltreatment whilst in the hands of the police.

In July 1964 another series of investigations stemmed from the activities of a detective sergeant in the metropolitan police in whom overwork had precipitated a mental breakdown and whose activities appeared to have included the fabrication of evidence in an indeterminate number of cases. Under the provisions of the Police Act the Home Secretary was able to set up a statutory inquiry into the circumstances in which it was possible for this police officer to continue on duty. Other allegations of metropolitan police corruption followed and the chief constable of Wolverhampton held an inquiry. Yet another took place under Mr W. L. Mars-Jones, Q.C.

These independent inquiries which have been held into police

---

[1] Cmnd. 2319 (1963). Report by Mr Norman Skelhorn, Q.C. The evidence given at the inquiry was not published with the report though requests were made in the Commons for publication. See 695 H.C. Deb. 837-53 (15 May 1964).

matters, together with others which have not,[1] suggest several morals. One is that the expression 'complaint' in relation to the police is capable of covering a number of different sorts of grievance and it does not follow that the same procedure is equally suitable for resolving them all. An internal investigation which may be satisfactory where a single constable is concerned may fail to satisfy where an allegation involves a number of officers or a course of conduct in which senior police officers are alleged to be involved. An (admittedly extreme) illustration of the way in which an internal disciplinary procedure can become a mutal putting together of heads was supplied by the Sheffield case. The provisions in the Police Act for investigation by an officer from an outside force provide a way in which this sort of suspicion by complainants may be partially remedied, though the extent to which the procedure will be used will depend (apart from intervention by the Home Office) on chief constables, and these reports need not be published.

Another distinction is between the type of complaint which, if made out, constitutes a disciplinary or possibly a criminal offence, and the complaint which is about other forms of police behaviour or activity. In the first instance the complaints procedure has to be such as to fit into the disciplinary and criminal processes without subjecting the police to an unfairly heavy burden of double jeopardy. Police duties, as distinct from any other form of public service, are such that constables are extremely exposed to accusations and complaints, many of which are virtually certain to be unjust,

---

[1] Requests were made in 1963 by M.P.s and others for inquiries into, *inter alia*, the disciplinary affairs of Liverpool Police Force, and allegations that police pressure had been brought to bear on witnesses as to evidence given by them at the trial of Stephen Ward.

The practice of searching premises without either warrants or permission, criticized in the Skelhorn Report, was also raised in the House when the Home Secretary was asked to institute an inquiry into the circumstances in which such a search had been allegedly made. The Home Secretary's reply on that occasion was that the Commissioner had informed him that consent had been obtained since the man concerned had been informed that it was intended to search his room and had raised no objection. The procedure in the Woolf case was comparable. See Cmnd. 2319 at p. 31 (Detective Sergeant Bell . . . had what he regarded as Mr Woolf's implied consent . . . Describing what he said when he first raised the matter with Mr Woolf [he] said 'I told him that I proposed to search his address').

insubstantial or malicious. Formal public tribunals for everything which can be called a 'complaint' would place a heavy burden on the police. In the procedure laid down in the Police Act there is the material for a fair balance between the realities of policing and the rights of the public in relation to the individual and disciplinary type of complaint. From the public's point of view, two essentials are a straightforward and sufficiently advertised method of registering a complaint and the expectation of a reasoned reply as to the decision taken. In cases which are investigated under the disciplinary regulations complainants will have this.

Where, however, complaints are made which do not relate to disciplinary offences or to the alleged misbehaviour of individual constables the picture is not so clear. The statutory procedure is obviously inappropriate where the 'complaint' relates to the activity or inactivity of the chief constable himself or to what has been done on his orders or on the orders of senior officers with his approval. The watch committee or police committee is the obvious recipient for such complaints. But there is no statutorily prescribed manner by which citizens can lay complaints before a watch committee. They may of course write letters to the chairman or to the Town Clerk, but watch committees are under no formal obligation to receive complaints, or if they do receive and discuss them, to inform complainants what action if any has been taken or whether there is thought to be any substance in the complaint submitted.

Here what is being complained about may be a mixed question of individual police behaviour and police policy. A good example is provided by the allegations made in September 1961 about the metropolitan police's handling of a demonstration in Trafalgar Square. Criticism levelled at the police related in part to the overall handling of the situation. It was alleged that the Commissioner had purported to exercise powers he did not possess, that demonstrators had been treated with unnecessary violence and that there had been attempts to prevent press and television reporters from recording what took place. In a debate in the House of Lords on 19 October, Lord Kilbracken said that he had observed what happened after midnight in the Square. A large force of constables had fallen on the few hundred remaining demonstrators, acting, he supposed, in a collective way, and in accordance with orders. Demonstrators had been dragged by the feet across the Square. Some of them had been thrown into the fountains.[1]

On this occasion the Home Secretary declined to set up an independent inquiry and stated that the Commissioner of Police was investigating fifty-four specific complaints about incidents in the Square and afterwards at police stations. On 1 March 1962 Mr Butler stated in the House that all the complaints had been investigated by senior officers not concerned in the incidents. Statements had been taken from over four hundred police officers and the Commissioner had concluded that the great majority had acted properly and with restraint. Towards the end of the operation, however, there appeared to have been a few cases in which some officers had fallen short of this standard. Four or five individuals had been put in the fountains (laughter). Unfortunately the most searching inquiries had failed to reveal the particular officers. A police sergeant had been admonished for allowing a hose to be turned on in the yard at Bow Street and a woman police sergeant had been admonished for a remark to which objection could be taken.[2]

This somewhat allusive report was precisely of the kind which is unlikely to satisfy complainants who feel that the police are investigating and may be whitewashing themselves. Here the reputation of the force was at stake to a greater extent than in many cases involving allegations of assault by police. It was a case in which an inquiry by an independent person with a full report would have been a reasonable measure. There was at least as much justification for such a form of inquiry as in the Woolf case. The Skelhorn and Mars-Jones Reports with their detailed accounts of the inquiries made and the reasons for their conclusions make a strong contrast with the process with which Mr Butler satisfied himself in 1961.

[1] 234 H.L. Deb. 627–35.   [2] 654 H.C. Deb. 5s. cols. 1537–8.

INDEPENDENT INVESTIGATION OF COMPLAINTS

At the Committee stage of the Police Bill proposals were put forward and rejected for panels of independent persons to review complaints against the police. A minority of the members of the Royal Commission, it will be remembered, suggested an independent 'ombudsman' or 'Commissioner of Rights' for the police.[1] Clearly some complaints are of such a kind that internal investigation which is satisfactory for many routine cases becomes open to objection and this fact is acknowledged by the setting up from time to time by the Home Secretary of independent inquiries and by the provision for them in the Police Act. At the same time such a process leaves it in the hands of the Home Secretary to decide whether independent inquiry is necessary and past experience suggests that where political feelings are aroused the discretion of the Home Secretary in deciding whether or not to expose senior police officers to a formal independent inquiry is not universally acceptable. What, if it could be devised, would seem right in principle would be an institutionalized procedure for inquiry which whilst completely independent of the police or Home Office would be flexible enough to arrange formal hearings only in appropriate cases. Some interesting experiments in procedures of this kind have been carried out in the United States.[2] In New York City, for example, non-uniformed officers of a special branch of the force known as the 'public relations division' deal with complaints. Completely independent complaints branches are rare, but at least two forces (Rochester, N.Y., and Philadelphia) have complaints bodies staffed by civilians unconnected with the police. The Philadelphia Complaints Review Board had in 1964 eight members reflecting legal, academic, religious and labour interests. Complaints must be lodged within ninety days at the Board's office, housed in buildings separated from those of the police department. There is an executive secretary who either attempts an informal settlement or

---

[1] See above, Chap. 5. Reference of complaints to magistrates has also been suggested. (See *Police Review*, 13 March 1964.)

[2] A survey, recently made, was published in the *Harvard Law Review* in 1964 under the title *The Administration of Complaints by Civilians against the Police* (72 H.L.R. 499).

forwards complaints to the police Commissioner. The Commissioner, whilst free to refuse to investigate, normally supplies a report and on the basis of this a legal sub-committee of the Complaints Board decides whether a formal hearing is necessary. In any adversary hearing police officers normally have legal representation. The system meets the demand of flexibility in that many informal settlements are arranged and the adversary hearing procedure is not used for minor complaints. Moreover, the Board need not intervene in the internal procedures of the police unless they feel it necessary and the full disciplinary and executive power remains in the hands of the police Commissioner to whom the Board can only make recommendations as to disciplinary action. It has been stated by the police that their morale has been in no way undermined by the Board's activities. One judgment on the system is that the Board 'has been able to supply citizens' judgment to police policies and activities. Where the question of drawing the proper boundary between effective law enforcement and the protection of civil liberties is involved, it seems proper that independent citizen judgment be given a formal role.'[1]

There is a great similarity between the arguments used against the introduction of independent bodies here and the arguments used in the general field of administration against the setting up of supervisory or inquiry procedures, namely that the public servants involved will be demoralized and their activities obstructed. This was the argument urged against the setting up of the Select Committee on Nationalized Industries and it is an argument frequently produced against the introduction of the 'ombudsman' or 'Commissioner of Rights' scheme for the investigation of grievances in administration. In Scandinavia and in New Zealand, where a general scheme of grievance investigation by a parliamentary Commissioner has been set up, no evidence of demoralization in the public service has been noted. A flexible but formal and independent complaints machinery with authority to reject frivolous, trivial or vexatious complaints is in fact a protection for public servants against unjust or misdirected criticism and, though first opposed by the civil

[1] 72 H.L.R. 499 at 513.

services in those countries, has come to be welcomed. When the promised Parliamentary Commissioner system is set up in Britain one function which the Commissioner might perform would be to advise the Home Secretary when it would be appropriate for an independent inquiry into police matters to be held. The Commissioner can hardly himself be burdened with all local police complaints. Here the more promising line of development appears to be in the direction of local machinery of the American kind.

POLICE POLICIES

But complaints may be about policy matters and it can be seen that the Police Act does not really acknowledge the necessity to provide for what the Royal Commission called the right of 'challenge to police policies'. Two points in the Commission's report are worth recalling here.[1] First, it was pointed out that the chief constables in their evidence had given a 'partial but inadequate recognition' to the fact that they were concerned with other matters besides the enforcement of the law in particular cases, namely with a range of decisions as to enforcement policies 'in matters which vitally concern the public interest'. Secondly, the Commissioners suggested, it could not be held that duties of this kind required 'the complete immunity from external influence necessary in the enforcement of the law in particular cases'. The Government have not accepted the logic of this proposition (and indeed the Commission itself failed to follow it out). This failure to provide effective means for challenging police policies, though a product of a particular constitutional doctrine, also appeals to a normal and optimistic assumption underlying many of our arrangements – namely that law and order is 'non-political'. Legal machinery, we like to feel, is both a part of and yet separate from the machinery of politics and government. This, in some ways peculiar, belief rests upon the existence of a settled constitution and a stable society and it most obviously tends to break down when the law is put into operation to enforce policies which are the subject of strong moral or political disagreements within society. The suffragette movement, fascist public meetings and

[1] See pp. 30–32 of the Report.

nuclear disarmament demonstrations provide examples. It is in fact parliamentary responses to questions of public order and security which in the twentieth century have placed in the hands of public officers, including the police, many discretionary, and in a sense political, powers which in earlier times were less evident. The Public Order Act of 1936, for example, gave chief constables power to regulate processions and to forbid them entirely for a period not exceeding three months by making an order to be approved by the local authority and the Home Secretary. This is essentially a form of preventive justice and is obviously discretionary in its nature, though the discretion is exercised in conjunction with an elected body and with the Secretary of State (who could presumably always have been asked in the House of Commons why he had given or refused his assent to an order made under the Public Order Act).

This Act itself is important in another way. Taken together with the power to prosecute for an obstruction of the police in the execution of their duty, it has lessened the importance of the old distinction between legal and illegal assemblies. If the purpose of assembling is politically or industrially controversial, or disliked by other sections or groups of people, there is often room for apprehension that there will be a breach of the peace which it is the duty of those in authority to prevent. Standards may vary when flexible concepts such as potential breaches of the peace, 'obstruction' or 'insulting behaviour' are concerned, and difficult decisions may have to be made by junior police officers at short notice. The National Council for Civil Liberties suggested to the Royal Commission that it was not unknown for constables whose directions were questioned at times of stress to use such phrases as 'Are you obstructing me in my duty?' or 'If you speak to me I'll arrest you'. Even if disorder is not imminent it is practically impossible for police decisions to be queried on the spot except by disobedience which is almost bound to lead to a breach of the law. Powers to deal with obstruction of the police are necessary but they may be used with varying degrees of intensity, especially where picketing or political activities are concerned, and the way in which the police regulate political demonstrations or processions has not always been consistent either as between one time and another or as between one organization and another.

The Official Secrets Acts have also added to the number of discretionary powers. Justices and superintendents of police, for example, may issue warrants to enter at any time any premises and to search and seize any person found there, along with any documents also on the premises which provide evidence of an offence under the Act. Offences under the Act are not all delineated with the precision usually found in British criminal legislation. No sketch, plan, model or note must be made, which is 'calculated to be, or might be, or is intended to be directly or indirectly useful to an enemy', active or potential. It is also provided by Section One of the principal Act, that an offence may be committed by a person whose conduct or 'known character' indicates a purpose prejudicial to the safety or interests of the state, though he is not shown to have committed any particular action. One cannot conceive a peacetime conviction on character grounds or for the possession of any one of the large number of documents which might be indirectly useful to the many potential enemies of the Crown; but it would be interesting to know what Dicey thought of the drafting of Section One when the Act of 1911 was passed.

A number of these powers have been used in the 1950s and 1960s. The Public Order Act and the powers of the Metropolitan Police Commissioner were invoked to control demonstrations by opponents of nuclear weapons. In 1962 warrants were issued under the Official Secrets Act to search and carry away files and papers on premises occupied by organizers of a civil disobedience campaign. A prosecution under the Act was instituted after an attempt to demonstrate at and enter a Royal Air Force station.[1] All these powers – of regulating and prohibiting, of laying informations, of issuing warrants – are powers of police or of justices, or indeed of private citizens. They are not directly powers of the Government.

Yet they are in a sense executive and governmental powers. A decision, say, to invoke the provisions of the Public Order Act, or to issue a series of warrants under the Official Secrets Acts, is essen-

[1] *Chandler v. D.P.P.*, [1962] 3 All E.R. 142.

tially a policy decision. Warrants of this kind would be normally executed by special branch officers acting under the directions of the Director of Public Prosecutions. On these matters the Attorney-General and the Director may properly seek advice from their ministerial colleagues, and the Cabinet is certainly within its rights in discussing with the Attorney-General the questions of public policy involved in law enforcement, and even the institution and withdrawal of proceedings in cases involving public order and security. Since the unfortunate withdrawal of the Campbell prosecution in 1924 it has been thought (probably wrongly) that in these matters the Law Officers may not be given instructions. But the Attorney-General and the Cabinet are accountable to Parliament, and Parliament is entitled to discuss the issues and if necessary to challenge the decisions. They may indeed be highly debatable and there is no sense in pretending that political and administrative judgment is not involved, or that the application of the law is an automatic process[1] for which no one need take responsibility.

Thus even in the prosecution and investigation of particular cases policy considerations may arise. Comment was attracted in 1963, for example, by the intensity of the investigations made by the police into the affairs of Stephen Ward in the aftermath of the Profumo Affair. It seems fairly clear from Lord Denning's report that the exceedingly large number of witnesses interviewed[2] and the enthusiasm of the police were the indirect result of executive decisions at a high level. That is not to say that the decisions were wrong or that it was improper to take them. They were, however, discretionary decisions which did not happen as automatic processes within an immunized sphere labelled 'the Machinery of Justice',

[1] In 1951 Sir Hartley Shawcross speaking as Attorney-General said in the Commons, 'It has never been the rule in this country . . . that suspected criminal offences must automatically be the subject of prosecution. The public interest . . . is the dominant consideration.' See 483 H.C. Deb. 5s. col. 679 et seq.

[2] In *The Trial of Stephen Ward*, at p. 238, Mr Ludovic Kennedy writes: 'The impression I gained of the police during the trial was that they were out to get Ward convicted . . . They interviewed on their own admission between 125 and 140 potential witnesses. It would be interesting to know the average number of potential witnesses interviewed in connection with similar charges during, say, the last five years: I doubt if they would run even into double figures.'

sealed off from all considerations of politics and public policy or even governmental expediency. Similarly a decision may sometimes be taken to prosecute a particular person or persons rather than others who might also have been proceeded against. This may be an inevitable form of executive choice. But it is a choice. It was thrown into relief during the trial at the Central Criminal Court in February 1962 of six members of the Campaign for Nuclear Disarmament when other members of the movement circulated a leaflet stating that they were equally guilty of offences under the Official Secrets Acts and that the Government was 'not prepared to apply the law impartially and has preferred to prosecute six individuals'.

The day-to-day business of prosecuting offences up and down the country is, in fact, shot through with discretion. Sometimes in a number of more serious offences the consent of the Director of Public Prosecutions or the Attorney-General may have to be obtained but over the greater part of the field the decisions are those of chief constables and senior police officers. There will be choices to be made in many cases – particularly road traffic offences – between prosecuting and issuing warnings. The existence of a police discretion of this kind[1] was made clear in 1963 by the chief constable of Southend, who stated that he would not in certain conditions necessarily prosecute for shoplifting offences. (The matter was raised in the House of Lords and some of their Lordships wondered what the views of the Southend watch committee and Southend shoplifters might be.) Again one of the Royal Commission's comments was on the lack of uniformity in the enforcement of the Road Traffic Acts. The point is borne out by the annual Home Office statistics of motor vehicle offences. In 1961 for example, Manchester prosecuted 4,569 motorists for obstruction and parking offences, Liverpool 1,386. For neglect of other traffic directions and prescribed route directions Manchester had 6,747 prosecutions as against 987 in Liverpool. Noting these figures the *Police Review* suggested that they were too great to be accounted for by variations

---

[1] For a comparative view of some American enforcement problems, see J. Goldstein, *Police Discretion not to enforce the Criminal Process*, 69 Yale Law Journal 543.

in local traffic conditions and that 'the policy of law enforcement adopted by the forces concerned must be primarily responsible'.[1]

In a society where obstruction of the highway is a fairly universal phenomenon the power to prosecute for it offers a number of opportunities for action or inaction. It is possible to adopt a different attitude towards, for example, large-scale obstruction for trade or commercial purposes (say by unloading vans or lorries) from that adopted towards smaller obstructions by political meetings,[2] processions or sellers of pamphlets or newspapers. There is often a choice of statutes under which proceedings may be brought. No intelligent police officer, as Sir Ivor Jennings has pointed out, would choose to prosecute for the offence of unlawful assembly rather than for obstructing the police. In the field of prosecution of obscene literature various forms of proceeding may be taken and the question whether to proceed at all and against what involves a certain amount of moral, aesthetic and political discrimination.

In the making of all these decisions judgment and policy may be sound or usually sound. It is in each case, however, a conceivable possibility that judgment may be open to criticism or unwise or even disastrously foolish. It is necessary to invoke the extreme and unlikely possibilities of misjudgment, inconsistency, partiality or abuse of discretion only to enable the point to be made that even the individual instance of prosecution or law enforcement is often not a straightforward matter of applying a rule of law. One cannot therefore defend a rationale of police independence from control or instructions simply on the ground that in enforcing the law there should be responsibility only to the law. Ex hypothesi, the discretionary decisions in question are all within the law and within the law there is no sense in which the law imposes responsibility or corrects error. The analogy with judicial independence is defective.

---

[1] *Police Review*, 2 November 1962.

[2] In *Arrowsmith v. Jenkins* brought under s.121 of the Highways Act, 1959, the Lord Chief Justice, dismissing an appeal from the magistrates, said, 'The appellant felt a grievance; why pick on her? Many meetings had been held in that street from time to time which the police had attended and assisted. There was no evidence of any prosecutions. That of course has nothing to do with this court.' (*The Times*, 7 March 1963.)

Although no one believes that judges exercise no discretion, their whole activity at least in principle is rule-governed. Political influence or orders directed to them would be inapt and improper because there is in principle a correct outcome to their procedure which is wholly contained in the applicable rules of law. In so far as equity or public policy influences their conduct, that too is contained in rules or principles. They are responsible to the law in the sense that the law in the shape of appellate tribunals will correct their mistakes.

The distinction between judicial and executive functions is of course only one of degree. Choice and discretion are always bounded within some limits. But in executive policy making the choice of principles is wider and less rule-bound. The principles themselves may include feelings of morality and common sense and when one executive decision is substituted for another it is not normally thought of as correcting it. It is on grounds of this kind that non-judicial decisions are exposed to criticism, argument and reversal.

If it is accepted that law enforcement may have aspects which place it closer to the executive than to the judicial function it cannot in its entirety demand the isolation and immunity accorded to purely judicial decision. What then ought ideally to be the relationship between those whose business it is to enforce the law and those whose business it is to supervise law enforcement and its ancillary activities. One principle which has been suggested is that the supervisory body or police authority should be competent to issue both advice and instructions of a general or policy character but not to intervene or issue instructions in individual cases. There is however a difficulty concealed in the expression 'individual cases'. An individual case may raise a question of policy. It may, for example, have unique or unexpected features or be an extreme instance of misjudgment. What would perhaps more accurately represent the feelings of those who have a principle of this kind in mind is that there ought not to be intervention in the *routine* individual case. If it displays no features requiring an exercise of special judgment then it should be dealt with as the routine or rules dictate or suggest.

We have seen that the argument about the actual powers of police and police authorities, as distinct from what might be advanced as a theoretically satisfactory relationship, has been complicated by the strongly entrenched, albeit recently inflated, legal doctrine about the office of constable. It has also been affected by fears about the dangers of party political contamination of the machinery of justice, and a distrust of the competence and capacity of local representative bodies. In the late nineteenth century it was such views which led some to feel that the Crown's role in the administration of justice as represented by the justices in quarter sessions could not be handed over entire to the new county councils elected on a widening franchise. In the 1960s the stoutest exponents of centralized administration must concede that the barriers against the abuse of power in police matters by locally elected bodies are adequate. The effective sanctions exercised by police authorities are subject to central approval by the Secretary of State who has in his hands, in addition, financial power and the powers of inspection and inquiry. In the face of these it can hardly be claimed that autonomy for chief constables is the only safeguard against political partiality, or improper interference in police matters. In the course of the proceedings on the Police Bill Government spokesmen, in fact, expressed the view that local watch committees had developed a strong immunity to internal political argument.

What then ought to be considered as the proper limits of intervention by police authorities in policing and law enforcement? A summary of the conclusions here reached would be as follows. First: an obvious limitation is that they cannot without exceeding their powers issue instructions which would involve a chief officer in a breach of a statutorily imposed duty or which would amount to a conspiracy on their own part to pervert the course of justice.

Secondly: in matters affecting the institution and withdrawal of prosecutions their powers as police authority should not be regarded as essentially different from those of the Home Secretary as police authority for the metropolitan area. As a matter of strong convention and sound administrative practice, intervention in routine prosecution matters should be excluded. There may, however, be

119

exceptions which cannot be set out in any simple formula. They may relate to particular policies adopted in the prosecutions of offences or exceptional particular cases. In all except the most extreme cases intervention would be expected to take the form of advice rather than a specific instruction. In extreme cases, however, instructions ought not to be ruled out, and no general legal principle does rule them out.

Thirdly: in matters, other than the institution of prosecutions, which affect the disposition of police forces, the methods used in policing and the enforcement of the law, administrative morality ought to restrict intervention in a chief constable's sphere of decision. But it is in this sphere, particularly, that executive decisions may be made and policies followed which ought on at least some occasions to be open to an effective challenge by the public and their elected representatives issuing where necessary in police authority directions.

It is clear enough that these principles cannot be reconciled with the views of recent Secretaries of State or with the legal thesis about the status of constables which has found favour in the last thirty years. That thesis, exaggerated and inconsistent as it is, remains a hardy one and it has almost taken on the character of a new principle of the constitution whilst nobody was looking. The spirit of *Fisher v. Oldham* can still be observed in the provisions of the new police legislation of 1964. We have argued that it implies a rationally indefensible relationship between the functions of police and government.

Judges' Rules and Administrative Directions to the Police, 1964

The Judges' Rules provide an example of what is in effect a form of administrative instruction to the police as to the manner in which they carry out their duties. It is, however, insisted that the rules are merely issued for the guidance of the police on the authority of the judges and the Note to the new rules states that the Judges 'do not control or in any way . . . supervise police activities or conduct'. Yet the rules themselves must surely be regarded in practice as regulating the conduct of police officers and they are certainly expressed in the imperative mood ('He shall caution . . .', 'a record shall be kept . . .' etc.). Since the rules are not rules of law and their violation does not necessarily render evidence inadmissible, it was possible to regard the old rules not as injunctions or prohibitions as to police conduct in itself but merely as a set of principles for obtaining evidence likely to be admissible. The issuing of additional administrative directions intimately connected with the application of the rules (such as those relating to display of notices at police stations and the prohibition on dispensing alcoholic refreshment) is not really compatible with this view. The old rules it may be noticed were described in *R. v. Voisin* [1918] 1 K.B. 531 as 'administrative directions *the observance of which the police authorities should enforce upon their subordinates* as tending to the fair administration of justice' (italics added).

On 16 March 1961 the Home Secretary, in a written answer in the House of Commons, said that he had consulted with both the Lord Chief Justice and the chairman of the Royal Commission on the Police and the Lord Chief Justice had agreed that the judges should carry out a review of the scope and operation of the Judges' Rules. The chairman of the Royal Commission had agreed to make available for this purpose any relevant material that came to the Commission's notice.[1] A more informal account of the origins of the operation was given in the Commons in 1963. 'We were told,' one member of the Commission said, 'that the Judges' Rules were out: that the judges had discussed the matter and had said that the Judges' Rules were made by judges. It is quite true that they made the last Judges' Rules and made pretty well a hash of them – and insisted that it was part of their prerogative. We were asked gracefully to give way and we gave way as gracefully as we could.'[2] Thus the Royal Commission, unlike their predecessors in 1929, did not discuss the Judges' Rules at all. Nor was there any opportunity for them to be discussed in Parliament before being promulgated. The new rules were published in the form of a Home Office circular[3] on 24 January 1964 and came into operation three days later (the police being audibly disgruntled at the short notice and lack of opportunity for rehearsal).

Revision of the rules was needed partly because some contained ambiguities and partly because it was thought by many that the old rules unduly hampered police questioning. Increasing public preoccupation with police matters and the state of crime had in fact attracted a number of criticisms – not all consistent – of the investigatory process. In 1960, for example, *Justice*, the British Branch of the International Commission of Jurists, published the results of a private inquiry entitled *Preliminary Investigations of Criminal Offences*. On police questioning opinions were divided. Mr (now Sir) John Foster, Q.C., in a dissenting contribution, argued that the Judges' Rules protected the criminal undeservedly. He added: 'The rule that the suspect must be cautioned when the police have made up their mind to arrest[4] seems to me contrary to common sense and the suspect in my view should not be cautioned

[1] 636 H.C. Deb. 5s. col. 145.   [2] 685 H.C. Deb. 5s. cols. 125–6 (Mr Hale).
[3] H.O. 31/1964.
[4] The rule did not in fact mention arrest, but a decision 'to charge a person with a crime'.

and should be told, if he objects to being questioned, that he is required to answer.'[1] The majority of the Report's authors did not however concur in this proposal and the judges have not adopted any modification of the kind, though they have offered to the police more scope for questioning suspects, subject to certain provisos.

Under the old rules it was the duty of a police officer to caution any person whom he had made up his mind to charge before putting further questions to him. Though the point was not clearly specified in the rules, persons in custody[2] were not to be cross-examined[3] about the offence with which they had been charged, and if making a voluntary statement were only to have such questions put to them as might remove ambiguities, for example as to times or places mentioned in their statement. It was not easy to see, in fact, what under the old rules the 'further questions' might properly be which seemed to be envisaged in the rule providing for caution. For at that stage, in a phrase of Lord Devlin's, the 'suspect' had already become the 'accused'. ('Whenever the evidence in the possession of the police has become sufficiently weighty to justify a charge the charge is for this purpose treated as having been made and the suspect is thereafter treated as the accused.'[4]) In other words, given that persons who have been charged should not be cross-examined and given that when there was enough evidence to caution there was, by definition, enough evidence to charge, there could be nothing to justify questioning in the notionally non-existent interval between caution and charge?[5]

Strictly followed, the rules must have placed difficulties in the

[1] *Op. cit.*, p. 27.

[2] Itself a term of uncertain meaning. See Brownlie, 'Police Questioning, Custody and Caution', 1960 *Criminal Law Review* 298. Cf. *R. v. Bass* [1953] I Q.B. 680.

[3] Though statutory obligations to answer questions have been created by the Official Secrets Acts and the Road Traffic Acts.

[4] *The Criminal Prosecution in England*, p. 29.

[5] It may have been arguable that questioning might take place after arrest, but before charge if these did not coincide. But in *R. v. Knight and Thayre*, (1905) 20 Cox C.C. 711, it was said '. . . the moment you have decided to charge him *and practically get him into custody*, then, in as much as a judge even can't ask a question, or a magistrate, it is ridiculous to suppose that a policeman can' (italics added). See also R. C. Cross and N. Wilkins, *An Outline of the Law of Evidence*, Chap. 11.

way of some forms of investigation. A crime may be committed by a group of people. Recent bank and train robberies provide obvious examples. Questioning of one suspect may be the best method of obtaining information leading to the arrest of others. But if there happened to be sufficient evidence to justify charging the suspect in question, the rules implied that he should be charged and the opportunity of questioning forgone. Police officers must frequently have been in the position of having to choose between either forgoing such opportunities and charging at the correct point in time or taking them and delaying the charge until an improperly late stage. It is true that, literally construed, the rules did not forbid such a procedure. They told the police officer to caution when he had made up his mind to charge but they did not remind him that he ought so to make up his mind when the information given him was sufficient for the purpose. However an officer who delayed a charge in such a way might later find himself cross-examined on the point. The preamble to the new Judges' Rules remedies the omission and explicitly states the principle that a charge should be preferred without delay as soon as there is enough evidence to justify it. The rules themselves attempt to ease the consequent dilemma by providing a possibility of some further questioning after the charge and caution.

Taking the new rules in sequence the most striking feature is their provision for an additional caution to be administered earlier than under the old practice. Besides being cautioned when there is sufficient evidence to charge him a suspect must now also be cautioned as soon as there are 'reasonable grounds for suspecting' that he has committed an offence. If the police wish to put certain questions they must also issue a third caution. In such circumstances a person cautioned when reasonably suspected, cautioned when charged and cautioned before being questioned will have been told three times[1] that he need say nothing. It seems quite likely that some potentially talkative offenders will feel that they can take a hint.

[1] A fourth caution may have to be given if a person questioned under Rule 3 is later shown a statement by another person charged with the same offence and wishes to comment on it. (See Rule 5.)

Relatively law-abiding people may also turn out to be something less than enthusiastic when faced with the cautions to which they are now entitled. The new rules provide for a caution where a person is either charged with *an offence* or informed that he may be prosecuted for it and official propriety may well be taken for improper officiousness. Sometimes (it has been pointed out) the citizen concerned may be in custody. But 'sometimes he will be an erring motorist conducting one of those terse conversations through the driver's window of a car. Sometimes he may even be a boy who has been playing street football. They are all now entitled specifically to be told that they are not obliged to say anything about their infirm windscreen-wipers, their unlit cycle lamps, their collarless dogs, unless they wish to do so, but that whatever they wish to say about these things will be 'taken down in writing and may be used in evidence'.[1] It may be that the rules will be applied in practice not to every breach of the criminal law but only to offences for which there is a power of arrest, or to indictable offences. But the rules do not say so.

Constables are now called upon to draw some rather delicate distinctions, which at points might strain the capacities of moral philosophers. First of all, they are told in Rule 1 that they are entitled to question anyone at all 'suspected or not' when trying to discover whether or by whom an offence has been committed. This is so, it is added, whether or not the person in question has been taken into custody, so long as he has not been charged with the offence or warned that he may be prosecuted. The implication of this is unclear. One explanation would be that the reference to a person in custody is to custody resulting from some other offence. If a person is in custody for the offence to which the questions relate he can hardly fall under the second part of the description 'suspected or not'. He may however be a person who is suspected but who cannot be questioned without detaining or arresting him. This has led some commentators to suggest that the new rules permit a hitherto unrecognized activity – namely detention for questioning.[2] What on this view is envisaged would seem to be

[1] *Police Review*, 31 January 1964.   [2] See L. H. Hoffman, 7 *The Lawyer* 23, at p. 26.

that a suspected person may be prevented from leaving a police station, in effect by arrest, and be questioned, provided that he is suspected enough to be given some general indication of the charge in accordance with the principle laid down in *Christie v. Leachinsky*.[1] Presumably questioning under these conditions would entail reasonable suspicion and hence the administering of the first caution. But whether it is permissible at all might be doubted. Rule 1 states that persons in custody may be questioned provided that they have not been charged or informed that they may be prosecuted for the offence in question. It is difficult to see how a man who has been detained against his will and given the information about the offence required by *Christie v. Leachinsky* can fail to have been informed that he may be prosecuted for it, even if it can be said that he has not been formally charged. If the judges meant to authorize detention for questioning they would surely have said so in clearer terms than this. The phrase used in Rule 2 upon which the issuing of a caution depends also presents difficulties. It could be given a very wide or a narrower meaning. In police work almost anything, however trivial, may be a ground for suspicion in one sense of 'suspicion'. 'Suspecting that' however can be given a sense in which something more substantial would be implied before it could properly be said that there were reasonable grounds for suspecting that a person has committed an offence. Given one interpretation almost everybody whom there was reason to question or whose character was known to be bad would be entitled to a caution since the smallest degree of 'suspicion' may be reasonably entertained. 'Reasonable grounds for suspecting that X' is in fact ambiguous as between 'Grounds for a reasonably large amount of suspicion that X' and 'Reasonable grounds for any suspicion (however small) that X'.

After the first caution a record must be kept of the time and place at which questioning or the making of a statement begins and ends and of the persons present. It is not stated that a record must be kept of the questions themselves. Nor is it said whether, if the suspect at that point makes a statement, the old restriction of cross-

[1] [1947] A.C. 573.

examination to the clearing up of ambiguities remains, or if cross-examination on the statement is permissible subject to the recording provisions made for the putting of questions.

If it is decided to charge the suspect with an offence or to warn of the possibility of prosecution the second caution must be given and further questions relating to the offence restricted (after the third caution) to what are described as 'exceptional cases'. Such questions as may be put are defined as those 'necessary for the purpose of preventing or minimizing harm or loss to some other person or to the public' or for clearing up ambiguity. This seems the only *quid pro quo* for the additional obligations imposed as to the cautioning of offenders. What it amounts to is as debatable as some other phrases in the rules. Anything which convicts the guilty prevents harm or loss to the public. A mild third degree or a vigorous police cross-examination might do so. Whether they are 'necessary' for the purpose is a matter of balancing what is gained against what is lost, including the possible rights of the accused and the general interests of justice. Nothing is simply 'necessary' to the end mentioned and the phrase here seems a difficult and question-begging one.

Taken all in all, the new Judges' Rules seem to demand even higher standards of forbearance, introspection and foresight than the old. It will be difficult to blame the police if they find these standards impossibly high.

JUDGES' RULES

NOTE

The origin of the Judges' Rules is probably to be found in a letter dated 26 October 1906, which the then Lord Chief Justice, Lord Alverstone, wrote to the Chief Constable of Birmingham in answer to a request for advice in consequence of the fact that on the same Circuit one Judge had censured a member of his force for having cautioned a prisoner, whilst another Judge had censured a constable for having omitted to do so. The first four of the present Rules were formulated and approved by the Judges of the King's Bench Division in 1912; the remaining five in 1918. They have been much criticized, *inter alia* for alleged lack of clarity and of efficacy for the protection of persons who are questioned by police officers; on the other hand it has been maintained that their application unduly hampers the detection and punishment of crime. A Committee of Judges has devoted considerable time and attention to producing, after consideration of representative views, a new set of Rules which has been approved by a meeting of all the Queen's Bench Judges.

The Judges control the conduct of trials and the admission of evidence against persons on trial before them: they do not control or in any way initiate or supervise police activities or conduct. As stated in paragraph (e) of the introduction to the new Rules, it is the law that answers and statements made are only admissible in evidence if they have been voluntary in the sense that they have not been obtained by fear of prejudice or hope of advantage, exercised or held out by a person in authority, or by oppression. The new Rules do not purport, any more than the old Rules, to envisage or deal with the many varieties of conduct which might render answers and statements involuntary and therefore inadmissible. The Rules merely deal with particular aspects of the matter. Other matters such as affording reasonably comfortable conditions, adequate breaks for rest and refreshment, special procedures in the case of persons unfamiliar with the English language or of immature age or feeble understanding, are proper subjects for administrative directions to the police.

JUDGES' RULES

These Rules do not affect the principles

(a) That citizens have a duty to help a police officer to discover and apprehend offenders;

(b) That police officers, otherwise than by arrest, cannot compel any person against his will to come to or remain in any police station;

(c) That every person at any stage of an investigation should be able to communicate and to consult privately with a solicitor. This is so even if he is in custody provided that in such a case no unreasonable delay or hindrance is caused to the processes of investigation or the administration of justice by his doing so;

(d) That when a police officer who is making inquiries of any person about an offence has enough evidence to prefer a charge against that person for the offence, he should without delay cause that person to be charged or informed that he may be prosecuted for the offence;

(e) That it is a fundamental condition of the admissibility in evidence against any person, equally of any oral answer given by that person to a question put by a police officer and of any statement made by that person, that it shall have been voluntary, in the sense that it has not been obtained from him by fear of prejudice or hope of advantage, exercised or held out by a person in authority, or by oppression.

The principle set out in paragraph (*e*) above is overriding and applicable in all cases. Within that principle the following Rules are put forward as a guide to police officers conducting investigations. Non-conformity with these Rules may render answers and statements liable to be excluded from evidence in subsequent criminal proceedings.

RULES

I. When a police officer is trying to discover whether, or by whom, an offence has been committed he is entitled to question any person, whether suspected or not, from whom he thinks that useful information may be obtained. This is so whether or not the person in question has been taken into custody so long as he has not been charged with the offence or informed that he may be prosecuted for it.

II. As soon as a police officer has evidence which would afford reasonable grounds for suspecting that a person has committed an offence, he shall caution that person or cause him to be cautioned before putting to him any questions, or further questions, relating to that offence.

The caution shall be in the following terms:

'You are not obliged to say anything unless you wish to do so but what you say may be put into writing and given in evidence.'

When after being cautioned a person is being questioned, or elects to make a statement, a record shall be kept of the time and place at which any such questioning or statement began and ended and of the persons present.

III—(*a*) Where a person is charged with or informed that he may be prosecuted for an offence he shall be cautioned in the following terms:

'Do you wish to say anything? You are not obliged to say anything unless you wish to do so but whatever you say will be taken down in writing and may be given in evidence.'

(*b*) It is only in exceptional cases that questions relating to the offence should be put to the accused person after he has been charged or informed that he may be prosecuted. Such questions may be put where they are necessary for the purpose of preventing or minimizing harm or loss to some other person or to the public or for clearing up an ambiguity in a previous answer or statement.

Before any such questions are put the accused should be cautioned in these terms:

'I wish to put some questions to you about the offence with which you have been charged (*or* about the offence for which you may be prosecuted).

You are not obliged to answer any of these questions, but if you do the questions and answers will be taken down in writing and may be given in evidence.'

Any questions put and answers given relating to the offence must be contemporaneously recorded in full and the record signed by that person or if he refuses by the interrogating officer.

(c) When such a person is being questioned, or elects to make a statement, a record shall be kept of the time and place at which any questioning or statement began and ended and of the persons present.

IV. All written statements made after caution shall be taken in the following manner:

(a) If a person says that he wants to make a statement he shall be told that it is intended to make a written record of what he says.

He shall always be asked whether he wishes to write down himself what he wants to say; if he says that he cannot write or that he would like someone to write it for him, a police officer may offer to write the statement for him. If he accepts the offer the police officer shall, before starting, ask the person making the statement to sign, or make his mark to, the following:

'I, ..., wish to make a statement. I want someone to write down what I say. I have been told that I need not say anything unless I wish to do so and that whatever I say may be given in evidence.'

(b) Any person writing his own statement shall be allowed to do so without any prompting as distinct from indicating to him what matters are material.

(c) The person making the statement, if he is going to write it himself, shall be asked to write out and sign before writing what he wants to say, the following:

'I make this statement of my own free will. I have been told that I need not say anything unless I wish to do so and that whatever I say may be given in evidence.'

(d) Whenever a police officer writes the statement, he shall take down the exact words spoken by the person making the statement, without putting any questions other than such as may be needed to make the statement coherent, intelligible and relevant to the material matters: he shall not prompt him.

(e) When the writing of a statement by a police officer is finished the person making it shall be asked to read it and to make any corrections, alterations or additions he wishes. When he has finished reading it he shall be asked to write and sign or make his mark on the following Certificate at the end of the statement:—

'I have read the above statement and I have been told that I can correct, alter or add anything I wish. This statement is true. I have made it of my own free will.'

(*f*) If the person who has made a statement refuses to read it or to write the above mentioned Certificate at the end of it or to sign it, the senior police officer present shall record on the statement itself and in the presence of the person making it, what has happened. If the person making the statement cannot read, or refuses to read it, the officer who has taken it down shall read it over to him and ask him whether he would like to correct, alter or add anything and to put his signature or make his mark at the end. The police officer shall then certify on the statement itself what he has done.

V. If at any time after a person has been charged with, or has been informed that he may be prosecuted for an offence a police officer wishes to bring to the notice of that person any written statement made by another person who in respect of the same offence has also been charged or informed that he may be prosecuted, he shall hand to that person a true copy of such written statement, but nothing shall be said or done to invite any reply or comment. If that person says that he would like to make a statement in reply, or starts to say something, he shall at once be cautioned or further cautioned as prescribed by Rule III (*a*).

VI. Persons other than police officers charged with the duty of investigating offences or charging offenders shall, so far as may be practicable, comply with these Rules.

ADMINISTRATIVE DIRECTIONS ON INTERROGATION AND THE TAKING OF STATEMENTS

1. *Procedure generally*

(*a*) When possible statements of persons under caution should be written on the forms provided for the purpose. Police officers' notebooks should be used for taking statements only when no forms are available.

(*b*) When a person is being questioned or elects to make a statement, a record should be kept of the time or times at which during the questioning or making of a statement there were intervals or refreshment was taken. The nature of the refreshment should be noted. In no circumstances should alcoholic drink be given.

(*c*) In writing down a statement, the words used should not be translated into 'official' vocabulary; this may give a misleading impression of the genuineness of the statement.

(*d*) Care should be taken to avoid any suggestion that the person's answers can only be used in evidence against him, as this may prevent an innocent person making a statement which might help to clear him of the charge.

2. *Record of interrogation*

Rule II and Rule III(*c*) demand that a record should be kept of the following matters:

(*a*) when, after being cautioned in accordance with Rule II, the person is being questioned or elects to make a statement – of the time and place at which any such questioning began and ended and of the persons present;

(*b*) when, after being cautioned in accordance with Rule III(*a*) or (*b*) a person is being questioned or elects to make a statement – of the time and place at which any questioning and statement began and ended and of the persons present.

In addition to the records required by these Rules full records of the following matters should additionally be kept:

(*a*) of the time or times at which cautions were taken, and

(*b*) of the time when a charge was made and/or the person was arrested, and

(*c*) of the matters referred to in paragraph 1(*b*) above.

If two or more police officers are present when the questions are being put or the statement made, the records made should be countersigned by the other officers present.

3. *Comfort and refreshment*

Reasonable arrangements should be made for the comfort and refreshment of persons being questioned. Whenever practicable both the person being questioned or making a statement and the officers asking the questions or taking the statement should be seated.

4. *Interrogation of children and young persons*

As far as practicable children (whether suspected of crime or not) should only be interviewed in the presence of a parent or guardian, or, in their absence, some person who is not a police officer and is of the same sex as the child. A child or young person should not be arrested, nor even interviewed, at school if such action can possibly be avoided. Where it is found essential to conduct the interview at school, this should be done only with the consent, and in the presence, of the head teacher, or his nominee.

5. *Interrogation of foreigners*

In the case of a foreigner making a statement in his native language:

(*a*) The interpreter should take down the statement in the language in which it is made.

(*b*) An official English translation should be made in due course and be proved as an exhibit with the original statement.

(*c*) The foreigner should sign the statement at (*a*).

Apart from the question of apparent unfairness, to obtain the signature of a suspect to an English translation of what he said in a foreign language can have little or no value as evidence if the suspect disputes the accuracy of this record of his statement.

6. *Supply to accused persons of written statement of charges*

(*a*) The following procedure should be adopted whenever a charge is preferred against a person arrested without warrant for any offence:

As soon as a charge has been accepted by the appropriate police officer the accused person should be given a written notice containing a copy of the entry in the charge sheet or book giving particulars of the offence with which he is charged. So far as possible the particulars of the charge should be stated in simple language so that the accused person may understand it, but they should also show clearly the precise offence in law with which he is charged. Where the offence charged is a statutory one, it should be sufficient for the latter purpose to quote the section of the statute which created the offence.

The written notice should include some statement on the lines of the caution given orally to the accused person in accordance with the Judges' Rules after a charge has been preferred. It is suggested that the form of notice should begin with the following words:

'You are charged with the offence(s) shown below. You are not obliged to say anything unless you wish to do so, but whatever you say will be taken down in writing and may be given in evidence'.

(*b*) Once the accused person has appeared before the court it is not necessary to serve him with a written notice of any further charges which may be preferred. If, however, the police decide, before he has appeared before a court, to modify the charge or to prefer further charges, it is desirable that the person concerned should be formally charged with the further offence and given a written copy of the charge as soon as it is possible to do so having regard to the particular circumstances of the case. If the accused person has then been released on bail, it may not always be practicable or reasonable to prefer the new charge at once, and in cases where he is due to surrender to his bail within forty-eight hours or in other cases of difficulty it will be sufficient for him to be formally charged with the further offence and served with a written notice of the charge after he has surrendered to his bail and before he appears before the court.

7. *Facilities for defence*

(*a*) A person in custody should be allowed to speak on the telephone to his solicitor or to his friends provided that no hindrance is reasonably likely to be caused to the processes of investigation, or the administration of justice by his doing so.

He should be supplied on request with writing materials and his letters should be sent by post or otherwise with the least possible delay. Additionally, telegrams should be sent at once, at his own expense.

(*b*) Persons in custody should not only be informed orally of the rights and facilities available to them, but in addition notices describing them should be displayed at convenient and conspicuous places at police stations and the attention of persons in custody should be drawn to these notices.

Police Act 1964
(Extract of main sections)

PART I

ORGANIZATION OF POLICE FORCES

County, county borough and combined forces

1.—(1) Subject to the provisions of this Act, a police force Police areas. shall be maintained for every county and county borough in England and Wales which is not comprised in the combined area constituted by an amalgamation scheme, and for every combined area constituted by such a scheme.

(2) For the purposes of this section, any detached part of a county which, immediately before the commencement of this Act, was policed by the police force of another county shall be treated as part of that other county.

(3) For the purposes of this section, any county borough the police force of which is consolidated with that of a county under a consolidation agreement shall, so long as that agreement continues in force, be treated as part of that county.

(4) For the purposes of this section, any part of a county which is for the time being comprised in the metropolitan police district shall be treated as not forming part of that county.

2.—(1) The police authority for a police area consisting of a Police county or county borough shall be a committee of the council authorities of the county or borough constituted in accordance with the for counties provisions of this section, to be known, in the case of a county, boroughs. as the police committee and, in the case of a borough, as the watch committee.

(2) The police committee for a police area consisting of a county shall consist of such number of persons as may be determined by the council of the county, and of that number—

(a) two thirds shall be members of the council of the county appointed by that council;

135

(b) one third shall be magistrates for the county appointed by the court of quarter sessions for the county.

(3) The watch committee for a police area consisting of a county borough shall consist of such number of persons as may be determined by the council of the borough, and of that number—

    (a) two thirds shall be members of the council of the borough appointed by that council;

    (b) one third shall be magistrates appointed by the magistrates for the borough from among their own number.

(4) The magistrates to be appointed members of a police committee or watch committee shall be appointed at such times, in such manner and for such term as may be prescribed by rules made by the Secretary of State; and the other members of a police committee or watch committee shall be appointed at such times, in such manner and for such term and may from time to time be determined by the council responsible for appointing them.

(5) The quorum of a police committee or watch committee shall be such as may from time to time be determined by the council of the county or county borough.

(6) Subsection (4) of section 85 of the Local Government Act 1933 (membership of committees of local authorities) shall apply to a committee appointed under this section as it applies to any committee appointed under that section, and paragraphs 1, 2 and 4 of Part V of Schedule 3 to that Act (proceedings of local authorities) shall apply to a committee appointed under this section as they apply to a local authority and as if for any reference to that Act there were substituted a reference to this Act.

(7) Any proceedings by or against a committee appointed under this section shall be brought by or against the clerk of the council or town clerk as representing that committee.

3.—(1) The police authority for a combined area shall be the combined police authority constituted for the purpose in accordance with the provisions of the relevant amalgamation scheme; and every such authority shall, subject to subsection (4) of this section, be a body corporate by such name as may be prescribed by the scheme. *Police authorities for combined areas.*

(2) A combined police authority shall be appointed in such manner, and shall consist of such number of persons, as may be

prescribed by the amalgamation scheme; and of the number of persons so prescribed—

(a) two thirds shall be members of the constituent councils;
(b) one third shall be magistrates for the constituent areas.

(3) Provision may be made by an amalgamation scheme for applying, in relation to the constitution and proceedings of the combined police authority and in relation to the officers of that authority, any of the provisions of Parts II to IV of the Local Government Act 1933 subject to such modifications as may be prescribed by the scheme.

(4) If the constituent councils request that the combined police authority to be constituted by an amalgamation scheme should be a committee of one of those councils, the scheme shall constitute the combined police authority a committee of that council instead of a body corporate; and the provisions of Schedule 1 to this Act shall have effect with respect to such a scheme and a combined police authority so constituted.

4.—(1) It shall be the duty of the police authority for every police area for which a police force is required to be maintained by section 1 of this Act to secure the maintenance of an adequate and efficient police force for the area, and to exercise for that purpose the powers conferred on a police authority by this Act. *General functions of police authorities.*

(2) The police authority for every such police area shall, subject to the approval of the Secretary of State and to regulations under Part II of this Act, appoint the chief constable of the police force maintained by that authority and determine the number of persons of each rank in that force which is to constitute the establishment of the force.

(3) The police authority for any such police area may, subject to the consent of the Secretary of State, provide and maintain such buildings, structures and premises, and make such alterations in any buildings, structures or premises already provided, as may be required for police purposes of the area.

(4) The police authority for any such police area may, subject to any regulations under Part II of this Act, provide and maintain such vehicles, apparatus, clothing and other equipment as may be required for police purposes of the area.

(5) A combined police authority may, if so authorized by the amalgamation scheme, make arrangements with any constituent authority for the use by the combined police authority of the services of officers of the constituent authority and the making

137

of contracts and payments on behalf of the combined police authority by the constituent authority.

5.—(1) The police force maintained for a police area under section 1 of this Act shall be under the direction and control of the chief constable appointed under section 4(2) of this Act. Chief constables.

(2) The same person may, with the consent of the police authorities concerned, be appointed chief constable of more than one police force.

(3) The Secretary of State shall not approve the appointment as first chief constable of a combined force of any person other than the chief constable of a police force which ceases to exist in consequence of the formation of the combined force unless the Secretary of State is satisfied, having regard to the size and character of the combined force and any exceptional circumstances, that some other person should be appointed.

(4) Without prejudice to any regulations under Part II of this Act or under the Police Pensions Act 1948, the police authority, acting with the approval of the Secretary of State, may call upon the chief constable to retire in the interests of efficiency.

(5) Before seeking the approval of the Secretary of State under subsection (4) of this section the police authority shall give the chief constable an opportunity to make representations and shall consider any representations so made.

(6) A chief constable who is called upon to retire as aforesaid shall retire on such date as the police authority may specify or on such earlier date as may be agreed upon between him and the police authority.

6.—(1) In every police force maintained under section 1 of this Act there shall be a deputy chief constable, who shall have all the powers and duties of the chief constable— Deputy and assistant chief constables.

(a) during any absence, incapacity or suspension from duty of the chief constable;

(b) during any vacancy in the office of chief constable;

but shall not have power to act by virtue of this subsection for any continuous period exceeding three months except with the consent of the Secretary of State.

(2) The provisions of subsection (1) above shall be in addition to, and not in substitution for, any other enactment which makes provision for the exercise by any other person of the powers conferred by that enactment on a chief constable.

(3) The establishment of any such police force as aforesaid

may include one or more persons holding the rank of assistant chief constable.

(4) Appointments to the office of deputy chief constable, and appointments or promotions to the rank of assistant chief constable, shall be made, in accordance with regulations under Part II of this Act, by the police authority after consultation with the chief constable and subject to the approval of the Secretary of State.

(5) Subsections (2), (4), (5) and (6) of section 5 of this Act shall apply to a deputy chief constable, and subsections (4), (5) and (6) of that section shall apply to an assistant chief constable, as they apply to a chief constable.

7.—(1) The ranks which may be held in a police force maintained under section 1 of this Act shall be such as may be prescribed by regulations under Part II of this Act and the ranks so prescribed shall include, in addition to chief constable and assistant chief constable, the ranks of superintendent, inspector, sergeant and constable. *Other members of police forces.*

(2) Appointments and promotions to any rank below that of assistant chief constable in any such police force shall be made, in accordance with regulations under Part II of this Act, by the chief constable. . . .

11. Arrangements shall be made (whether by standing orders or otherwise) for enabling questions on the discharge of the functions of the police authority for any county, county borough or combined area to be put, in the course of the proceedings of the council for that county or county borough or, as the case may be, of a constituent council, by members of that council for answer by a member thereof who is also a member of the police authority and is nominated by that authority for that purpose. *Questions on police matters by members of county and county borough councils.*

General provisions

12.—(1) Every chief constable shall, as soon as possible after the end of each calendar year, submit to the police authority a general report in writing on the policing during that year of the area for which his force is maintained. *Reports by chief constables to police authorities.*

(2) The chief constable of a police force shall, whenever so required by the police authority, submit to that authority a report in writing on such matters as may be specified in the requirement, being matters connected with the policing of the area for which the force is maintained.

(3) If it appears to the chief constable that a report in compliance with any such requirement of the police authority would contain information which in the public interest ought not to be disclosed, or is not needed for the discharge of the functions of the police authority, he may request that authority to refer the requirement to the Secretary of State; and in any such case the requirement shall be of no effect unless it is confirmed by the Secretary of State.

(4) This section applies to the City of London police force as if for references to the chief constable here were substituted references to the Commissioner.

13.—(1) If it appears to the chief officers of police of two or more police forces that any police functions can more efficiently be discharged by members of those forces acting jointly, they may, with the approval of the police authorities for the areas for which those forces are maintained, make an agreement for that purpose.

Collaboration agreements.

(2) If it appears to any two or more police authorities that any premises, equipment or other material or facilities can with advantage be provided jointly for the police forces maintained by those authorities, they may make an agreement for that purpose.

(3) Any expenditure incurred under an agreement made under this section shall be borne by the police authorities in such proportions as they may agree or as may, in default of agreement, be determined by the Secretary of State.

(4) An agreement under subsection (1) or subsection (2) of this section may be varied or determined by a subsequent agreement.

(5) If it appears to the Secretary of State that an agreement should be made under subsection (1), subsection (2) or subsection (4) of this section, he may, after considering any representations made by the parties concerned, direct those parties to enter into such an agreement under those provisions as may be specified in the direction.

(6) The reference in subsection (1) of this section to members of a police force includes a reference to special constables for the area for which that force is maintained.

14.—(1) The chief officer of police of any police force may, on the application of the chief officer of police of any other police force, provide constables or other assistance for the purpose of enabling the other force to meet any special demand on its resources.

Aid of one police force by another.

(2) If it appears to the Secretary of State to be expedient in the interests of public safety or order that any police force should be reinforced or should receive other assistance for the purpose of enabling it to meet any special demand on its resources, and that satisfactory arrangements under subsection (1) above cannot be made, or cannot be made in time, he may direct the chief officer of police of any police force to provide such constables or other assistance for that purpose as may be specified in the direction.

(3) While a constable is provided under this section for the assistance of another police force he shall, notwithstanding section 5(1) of this Act, be under the direction and control of the chief officer of police of that other force.

(4) The police authority maintaining a police force for which assistance is provided under this section shall pay to the police authority maintaining the force from which that assistance is provided such contribution as may be agreed upon between those authorities or, in default of any such agreement, as may be provided by any agreement subsisting at the time between all police authorities generally, or, in default of such general agreement, as may be determined by the Secretary of State. . . .

18.—Every member of a police force maintained for a police area and every special constable appointed for a police area shall, on appointment, be attested as a constable by making a declaration in the form set out in Schedule 2 to this Act— *Attestation of constables.*

   (a) in the case of the metropolitan police district, before the Commissioner or an Assistant Commissioner of Police of the Metropolis;

   (b) in any other case, before a justice of the peace having jurisdiction within the police area.

19.—(1) A member of a police force shall have all the powers and privileges of a constable throughout England and Wales. *Jurisdiction of constables.*

(2) A special constable shall have all the powers and privileges of a constable in the police area for which he is appointed.

(3) Without prejudice to subsection (2) above, a special constable appointed for any police area shall have all the powers and privileges of a constable—

   (a) in the case of a police area not being a county borough, in any other police area which is contiguous to his own police area and in any police area being a county borough which is contiguous to any such other police area:

(b) in the case of a police area being a county borough, in any other police area which is contiguous to the borough and in any area in which special constables appointed for any such other police area have those powers and privileges by virtue of paragraph (a) above.

(4) A special constable who is for the time being required by virtue of section 13 or section 14 of this Act to serve with another police force shall have all the powers and privileges of a constable in any area in which special constables appointed for the area for which that force is maintained have those powers and privileges under this section.

(5) Subsection (3) of this section shall apply to the City of London as if it were a county borough; and for the purposes of that subsection in its application to special constables appointed for the metropolitan police district, the county of Berkshire shall be deemed to be contiguous to that district.

(6) This section is without prejudice to section 5 of the Police (Scotland) Act 1956 (execution of warrants in border counties of England and Scotland) and to any other enactment conferring powers on constables for particular purposes. . . .

Amalgamations

21.—(1) If it appears to the police authorities for any two or more police areas, being areas for which police forces are required by section 1 of this Act to be maintained, that it is expedient that those areas should be amalgamated for police purposes, they may for that purpose submit to the Secretary of State an amalgamation scheme, and the Secretary of State may by order approve any scheme so submitted to him.

(2) If it appears to the Secretary of State that it is expedient in the interests of efficiency that an amalgamation scheme should be made for any two or more such police areas and no scheme satisfactory to him has been submitted under subsection (1) of this section, the Secretary of State may for that purpose by order make such amalgamation scheme as he considers expedient.

(3) An amalgamation scheme shall make provision with respect to the following matters, that is to say—

(a) the establishment of a combined police authority and a combined police force for the combined area constituted by the scheme and of a combined police fund for the payment of the expenses of that authority and force;

Amalgamation schemes.

(*b*) the appointment of officers of the combined police authority, including a clerk of that authority and a treasurer of the combined police fund;

(*c*) the payment into the combined police fund, out of the local funds of the areas comprised in the combined area, of contributions assessed in accordance with the provisions of the scheme;

(*d*) the transfer for the purposes of the scheme of members of the police forces concerned, other than chief constables, and of special constables and police cadets;

(*e*) the transfer to the combined police authority of property, rights and liabilities of the constituent authorities, and officers of those authorities, or the use by the combined police authority of any such property;

(*f*) the delegation to the constituent councils of the functions of police authorities under section 5 of the Police, Factories etc. (Miscellaneous Provisions) Act 1916 and under the House to House Collections Act 1939;

and may provide for any other matters incidental to or consequential on the provisions of the scheme.

(4) Any functions which are delegated to a council by virtue of paragraph (*f*) of subsection (3) of this section may be delegated by that council to a committee of the council.

(5) An amalgamation scheme shall come into force on such date as may be prescribed by the scheme, and different dates may be so prescribed for the purposes of the provisions of the scheme relating to the constitution of the combined police authority and the performance by that authority of functions necessary for bringing the scheme into full operation, and for other purposes of the scheme.

(6) Before approving or making an amalgamation scheme the Secretary of State shall ascertain whether the constituent councils desire to make such a request as is referred to in section 3(4) of this Act.

(7) Schedule 3 to this Act shall have effect with respect to the procedure for making amalgamation schemes under subsection (2) of this section; and the transitory provisions set out in Schedule 4 to this Act shall have effect in relation to any amalgamation scheme under this section.

(8) A draft of any statutory instrument to be made under subsection (2) of this section shall be laid before Parliament. . . .

PART II

CENTRAL SUPERVISION,
DIRECTION AND FACILITIES

Functions of Secretary of State

28. The Secretary of State shall exercise his powers under this Act in such manner and to such extent as appears to him to be best calculated to promote the efficiency of the police.

General duty of Secretary of State.

29.—(1) The Secretary of State may require a police authority to exercise their power under Part I of this Act to call upon the chief constable to retire in the interests of efficiency.

Removal of chief constables etc.

(2) Before requiring the exercise of that power or approving the exercise of that or the similar power exercisable with respect to the deputy or an assistant chief constable, the Secretary of State shall give the chief constable or deputy or assistant chief constable an opportunity to make representations to him and shall consider any representations so made.

(3) Where representations are made under this section the Secretary of State may, and in a case where he proposes to require the exercise of the power mentioned in subsection (1) of this section shall, appoint one or more persons (one at least of whom shall be a person who is not an officer of police or of a Government department) to hold an inquiry and report to him and shall consider any report made under this subsection.

(4) The costs incurred by a chief constable or deputy or assistant chief constable in respect of an inquiry under this section, taxed in such manner as the Secretary of State may direct, shall be defrayed out of the police fund.

30.—(1) The Secretary of State may require any chief constable to submit to him a report on such matters as may be specified in the requirement, being matters connected with the policing of his area.

Reports from chief constables.

(2) Every chief constable shall, as soon as possible after the end of each calendar year, submit to the Secretary of State the like report as is required by subsection (1) of section 12 of this Act to be submitted to the police authority.

(3) This section shall apply to the City of London police force as if for references to a chief constable there were substituted references to the commissioner.

31.—(1) The Secretary of State may make grants in respect of expenses incurred for police purposes—

Police grant.

(a) by any police authority maintaining a county police

force, county borough police force or combined police force;

(b) by the Receiver for the Metropolitan Police District or by the Common Council of the City of London.

(2) Grants under this section shall be of such amounts, be payable at such times, in such manner, and subject to such conditions, and be carried to such funds, as the Secretary of State may with the approval of the Treasury by order determine; and any such order may provide for the deduction from grants under this section of such sums as may be determined by or under the order on account of expenditure of the Secretary of State under section 41, 44 or 45 of this Act.

(3) Any statutory instrument made under this section shall be subject to annulment in pursuance of a resolution of either House of Parliament.

(4) Any expenses incurred for the purpose of or in connection with the functions of a police authority under section 2 of the Road Traffic and Roads Improvement Act 1960 shall be treated for the purposes of this section as expenses incurred by that authority for police purposes.

32.—(1) The Secretary of State may cause a local inquiry to be held by a person appointed by him into any matter connected with the policing of any area. *Local inquiries.*

(2) Any inquiry under this section shall be held in public or in private as the Secretary of State may direct.

(3) Subsections (2) and (3) of section 290 of the Local Government Act 1933 (power to summon and examine witnesses) shall apply to any inquiry held under this section as they apply to an inquiry held under that section.

(4) Where the report of the person holding an inquiry under this section is not published, a summary of his findings and conclusions shall be made known by the Secretary of State so far as appears to him consistent with the public interest.

(5) The Secretary of State may direct that the whole or part of the costs incurred by any person for the purposes of any inquiry held under this section shall be defrayed out of the police fund or, if the inquiry relates to more than one police area, out of the police funds concerned in such proportions as may be specified in the direction; and any costs payable under this section shall be subject to taxation in such manner as the Secretary of State may direct.

33.—(1) Subject to the provisions of this section, the Secretary of State may make regulations as to the government, administration and conditions of service of police forces.

(2) Without prejudice to the generality of subsection (1) above, regulations under this section may make provision with respect to the following matters, that is to say:—

(a) the ranks to be held by members of police forces;

(b) the qualifications for appointment and promotion of members of police forces;

(c) periods of service on probation;

(d) voluntary retirement of members of police forces;

(e) the maintenance of discipline in police forces;

(f) the suspension of members of a police force from membership of that force and from their office as constable;

(g) the maintenance of personal records of members of police forces;

(h) the duties which are or are not to be performed by members of police forces;

(i) the treatment as occasions of police duty of attendance at meetings of the Police Federations and of any body recognized by the Secretary of State for the purposes of section 47 of this Act;

(j) the hours of duty, leave, pay and allowances of members of police forces; and

(k) the issue, use and return of police clothing, personal equipment and accoutrements.

(3) Regulations under paragraph (e) of subsection (2) above shall provide for the determination by the appropriate disciplinary authority of questions whether offences against discipline have been committed and for the punishment by that authority, by way of dismissal, requirement to resign, reduction in rank, reduction in rate of pay, fine, reprimand or caution, of any member of a police force who is found in the manner so provided to have committed any such offence; and for that purpose the appropriate disciplinary authority in respect of a police force maintained under section 1 of this Act shall be—

(a) in relation to the chief constable, deputy chief constable and any assistant chief constable, the police authority;

(b) in relation to any other member of any such police force, the chief constable:

Provided that in any case in which the chief constable is

146

interested otherwise than in his capacity as such, or in which he is a material witness, the appropriate disciplinary authority under paragraph (*b*) of this subsection shall be such other person or authority as may be prescribed by regulations under this section.

(4) Regulations under this section for regulating pay and allowances may be made with retrospective effect to any date specified therein, but nothing in this subsection shall be construed as authorizing pay or allowances payable to any person to be reduced retrospectively.

(5) Regulations under this section may make different provision for different cases and circumstances, and may authorize the Secretary of State to make provision for any purposes specified in the regulations.

(6) Any statutory instrument made under this section shall be subject to annulment in pursuance of a resolution of either House of Parliament. . . .

37.—(1) Subject to the provisions of this section, a member of a police force who is dealt with for an offence against discipline may appeal to the Secretary of State. *Disciplinary appeals.*

(2) On an appeal under this section the Secretary of State may make an order—

(*a*) allowing the appeal;
(*b*) dismissing the appeal; or
(*c*) varying the punishment by substituting some other punishment (whether more or less severe) which could have been imposed on the appellant.

(3) The Secretary of State may direct the appellant to pay the whole or any part of his own costs, but, subject to any such direction, all the costs and expenses of an appeal under this section, including the costs of the parties, shall be defrayed out of the police fund.

(4) If provision is made by or under regulations under section 33 of this Act entitling a member of the metropolitan police force to appeal against any decision to the Commissioner of Police of the Metropolis, no appeal shall lie under this section against that decision unless it has been affirmed or varied on such an appeal to the Commissioner.

(5) Schedule 5 to this Act shall have effect in relation to any appeal under this section.

Inspectors of constabulary

38.—(1) Her Majesty may appoint such number of inspectors (to be known as 'Her Majesty's Inspectors of Constabulary') as the Secretary of State may with the consent of the Treasury determine, and of the persons so appointed one may be appointed as chief inspector of constabulary. *Appointment and functions of inspectors of constabulary.*

(2) It shall be the duty of the inspectors of constabulary to inspect, and report to the Secretary of State on the efficiency of, all police forces maintained under section 1 of this Act and the City of London police force.

(3) The inspectors of constabulary shall carry out such other duties for the purpose of furthering police efficiency as the Secretary of State may from time to time direct.

(4) The chief inspector of constabulary shall in each year submit to the Secretary of State a report in such form as the Secretary of State may direct, and the Secretary of State shall lay a copy of that report before Parliament.

(5) The inspectors of constabulary shall be paid such salary and allowances as the Secretary of State may with the consent of the Treasury determine.

39.—(1) The Secretary of State may appoint assistant inspectors of constabulary, and may appoint members of police forces to be staff officers to the inspectors of constabulary. *Assistant inspectors and staff officers.*

(2) Persons appointed under this section shall be paid such salary and allowances as the Secretary of State may with the consent of the Treasury determine. . . .

PART IV

MISCELLANEOUS AND GENERAL

Remedies and complaints against police

48.—(1) The chief officer of police for any police area shall be liable in respect of torts committed by constables under his direction and control in the performance or purported performance of their functions in like manner as a master is liable in respect of torts committed by his servants in the course of their employment, and accordingly shall in respect of any such tort be treated for all purposes as a joint tortfeasor. *Liability for wrongful acts of constables.*

(2) There shall be paid out of the police fund—

148

(a) any damages or costs awarded against the chief officer of police in any proceedings brought against him by virtue of this section and any costs incurred by him in any such proceedings so far as not recovered by him in the proceedings; and

(b) any sum required in connection with the settlement of any claim made against the chief officer of police by virtue of this section, if the settlement is approved by the police authority.

(3) Any proceedings in respect of a claim made by virtue of this section shall be brought against the chief officer of police for the time being or, in the case of a vacancy in that office, against the person for the time being performing the functions of the chief officer of police; and references in the foregoing provisions of this section to the chief officer of police shall be construed accordingly.

(4) A police authority may, in such cases and to such extent as they think fit, pay any damages or costs awarded against a member of the police force maintained by them, or any constable for the time being required to serve with that force by virtue of section 14 of this Act, or any special constable appointed for their area, in proceedings for a tort committed by him, any costs incurred and not recovered by him in any such proceedings, and any sum required in connection with the settlement of any claim that has or might have given rise to such proceedings; and any sum required for making a payment under this subsection shall be paid out of the police fund.

49.—(1) Where the chief officer of police for any police area receives a complaint from a member of the public against a member of the police force for that area he shall (unless the complaint alleges an offence with which the member of the police force has then been charged) forthwith record the complaint and cause it to be investigated and for that purpose may, and shall if directed by the Secretary of State, request the chief officer of police for any other police area to provide an officer of the police force for that area to carry out the investigation. *Investigation of complaints.*

(2) A chief officer of police shall comply with any request made to him under subsection (1) of this section.

(3) On receiving the report of an investigation under this section the chief officer of police, unless satisfied from the report that no criminal offence has been committed, shall send the report to the Director of Public Prosecutions.

50. Every police authority in carrying out their duty with respect to the maintenance of an adequate and efficient police force, and inspectors of constabulary in carrying out their duties with respect to the efficiency of any police force, shall keep themselves informed as to the manner in which complaints from members of the public against members of the force are dealt with by the chief officer of police. . . .

Information as to manner of dealing with complaints.

A National Police Force: Two Views

27. The sixth principle is a negative one. The Commission has done a notable service by refuting the arguments that a national police force, whether organized on a regional basis or on a unitary one, would be either constitutionally objectionable or politically dangerous. Dicey, in his classic work on *The Law of the Constitution*, demonstrated that British liberty was based on the rule of law and on the supremacy of Parliament; it does not ever seem to have occurred to him that this freedom would be endangered if the separate and independent police forces were placed under central control. It is strange to find that those who most fear the police are the chief constables, for they expressed the view that a national police force would be a danger to liberty. Similarly Sir Frank Newsam, Permanent Under-Secretary, the Home Office, 1948-57, has said: 'The point which should be emphasized in this context is that, with the exception of the metropolitan police force, every police force is under local control, and that there is no danger of the police being used as the servants of the central authority.' It is odd to find an officer of the central authority expressing anxiety concerning the danger to liberty that would ensue if the central authority (the Home Secretary) had the power to give directions to police officers in regard to the enforcement of the law.

28. Although the Commission does not fear that the police, if placed under the direct control of the Government, would be dangerous, it nevertheless holds that this 'would be a notable constitutional change'. To extend the metropolitan police system to the other police forces in the country would not, however, be as radical a constitutional change as was introduced by Peel in 1829 when he abolished the parish constable and created the 'New Police'. For that matter it is doubtful whether such an extension of the metropolitan system to the provincial forces could properly be described as a constitutional change at all.

29. It has been suggested that the recent dictatorships on the Continent ought to be a warning against the establishment of a strong, centrally-controlled police force here. I believe that the lesson is the exact opposite. The danger in a democracy does not lie in a central police that is too strong, but in local police forces that are too weak. It was the private gangs of the Fascists and of the Nazis that enabled Mussolini and Hitler to establish their dictatorships when the legitimate police proved impotent.

LOCAL FORCES AND EFFICIENCY

30. The most important statement in the report is found in paragraph 22 which reads: 'If there had been evidence that a system based on a series of local forces was itself in some measure to blame for the inability of the police in the post-war years to halt the rise in crime . . . it would have been our duty to propose to Your Majesty a new system for the policing of this country. We have received no such evidence.'

31. This obviously does not mean that the Commission has reached the conclusion that there are no defects at the present time, because in paragraph 19 it finds that the existing system does not adequately (1) achieve the maximum efficiency and the best use of manpower, (2) bring the police to account, and so keep a constitutionally proper check upon mistakes and errors of judgment, and (3) arrange that complaints against the police are dealt with so as to avoid the present measure of dissatisfaction. But these defects, it holds, can be corrected by the recommendations it is making, so that it will not be necessary to alter the present system in the more radical manner suggested by those who favour a number of regional forces on the model of the metropolitan police.

32. The Commission places the major emphasis on the problem of maximum efficiency. In considering this it is essential to distinguish between (a) the efficiency of the individual police force, and (b) the efficiency of the police as a whole, in enforcing a national system of law and order. This distinction is an important one, because even though all the component parts of a machine may themselves be efficient, nevertheless the machine, considered as a single unit, may be unable to perform adequately the task for which it has been designed. As one witness said, a horse and a carriage may be kept in excellent condition, but nevertheless they may be too slow in the age of the motor vehicle.

33. In regard to the efficiency of the individual police forces the findings of the Commission itself are of great interest. These are that forces as small as 200 men tend to suffer a number of disadvantages, and that forces numbering less than 350 in strength are justifiable only in 'special circumstances'. There are 58 forces under 200 and 97 under 350 in strength, so that if 'special cir-

cumstances' has its usual meaning, more than half of the present forces fall short, and some fall far short of maximum efficiency. The disadvantages listed by the Commission are that these forces cannot meet all the demands that may be placed upon them, that the employment of specialists is difficult, that promotion tends to stagnate and it is harder, therefore, to ignore the claims of seniority, that discipline is difficult to enforce impartially and unpleasant in its effects, and that the risk of undesirable pressure being brought to bear on members of the force by local people is greater than in a large force. Nor is it easy to find for such a force a chief constable with all the necessary qualities of a leader. To this list of defects may be added the important one, which is found both in small and in large forces, that once a chief constable is appointed, then no change can be made unless he resigns or is found to be so grossly incompetent as to justify dismissal.

34. In face of this list of defects inherent in a small force the Commission has itself referred to a number of countervailing considerations. The first is that by amalgamation these small forces could be abolished so that only those of the optimum size of 500 or more would remain. This, however, would destroy the principal argument in favour of local forces which is based on their close relationship to the county or borough councils. Once this is gone it would obviously be more rational to plan the police on a regional basis. The second argument is that the loss of efficiency, which is inherent in the present system, is more than counterbalanced by the advantage that is gained by encouraging an interest in local government. Those who adopt this argument are prepared to pay the price of a less efficient police force, but this view is not necessarily a convincing one at a time when the number of crimes is rising at an appalling rate, with its inevitable repercussions on the moral standards of the country. Moreover if the police are to be used to increase the interest in local politics, then local politics will increase its interest in the police. The third argument is that as most crimes (more than 80 per cent) are committed by local people, it is an advantage that the police should be controlled by an independent local body which understands the local conditions. The truth of the statement that most crimes are local depends on what is meant by 'local', and also on whether the word 'crime' covers minor infractions of the law. Lord Geddes, Sir George Turner and Mr Hetherington have pointed out that in 1960 there were 743,713 serious crimes (an increase of 225 per cent over 1938), but that only 44.4 per cent were detected. It is therefore impossible to say whether 55.6 per cent of these crimes were committed by local people or not. The evidence seems to show that many of the serious crimes are of a non-local character. It is doubtful, therefore, whether the knowledge which members of a watch committee may have concerning local conditions will add greatly to the efficiency of the police in dealing with these crimes. More information concerning local crime can probably be obtained from public-

house keepers than from the members of a watch committee, but it does not follow that the former should become a police authority.

35. In regard to the efficiency of the police system as a whole the Commission recognizes that under modern conditions a certain amount of joint action on the part of various police forces is essential. This is most obvious in urban areas, but it is also true in less populous ones. The emphasis on crime squads and on traffic control are clear examples. If experience in other fields is any guide, it seems to be self-evident that such joint action can be more effectively achieved under a centralized control than under existing conditions, where the concurrence of the chief constables and of the local police authorities must be obtained. The Commission expresses the view that 'British experience in many fields of administration has shown that more can generally be achieved in the long run by persuasion than by compulsion'. This may be true in those instances where the persuasion is exerted by someone who also has the power to direct, but persuasion by itself is not always effective. An empty velvet glove is inclined to be flabby. A system of 'elaborate checks and counter-checks with the minimum of direction and command' to which the Commission refers is hardly a formula for successful administration.

36. It is of interest that the Commission has found that in regard to the large urban areas, known as conurbations, there is a case for considering whether each conurbation should be policed by a single police force. It recognizes that there are cogent arguments in favour of such a general amalgamation. There is the need to keep a routine check on criminals who live in one neighbourhood and operate in another; there is also the need to improve traffic control and secure its uniform enforcement. In a continuous urban area command is preferable to co-ordination as it can secure more efficient use of resources and greater flexibility. The same arguments apply, although with perhaps less obvious force, to non-urban areas, especially where there is no natural division between them. There is, therefore, strong evidence that a regional system would increase the efficiency of the police as a whole.

37. Finally, there is a third kind of efficiency which can be attained only by the exercise of increased Control by the Home Office. The Commission has set out a formidable list of matters for which the Home Secretary should be responsible, viz. effective execution by police authorities of their duties, efficiency of each separate police force, securing collaboration between groups of forces, and the provision of ancillary services, but it has not stated how he is to carry out these duties. At present the first three can be made effective only by a threat to withdraw the police grant, but this is such an indirect and clumsy method that it has rarely been threatened, and even more rarely used. The fourth matter which covers the provision of ancillary services has been more successfully carried out as these are usually under the direct control of the Home Office. . . .

EXTRACT FROM THE ASSOCIATION OF MUNICIPAL CORPORA-
TIONS' COMMENTS ON THE ROYAL COMMISSION'S REPORT

THE RELATIONSHIP BETWEEN THE SIZE AND THE
EFFICIENCY OF THE POLICE FORCES

15. The Commission considered that forces numbering less than 200 suffer considerable handicaps; that the retention of forces under 350 in strength is justifiable only in special circumstances, and that the optimum size of a police force is at least 500. Their reasons for this conclusion were based on opinions rather than facts, and the Association therefore endeavoured to do what the Commission did not attempt, namely to obtain the facts upon which firm conclusions can be based. This task has not been an easy one since several of the suggested disadvantages of small forces were so vague that they did not lend themselves to refutation by facts; others, however, can be proved or disproved, and we therefore sent a questionnaire to every city and borough in England and Wales with a separate police force, ranging in size from Dewsbury with a population of scarcely 53,000 and a force of 94, to Birmingham with a population of over 1,000,000 and a force of 2,174.

16. The first supposed disadvantage of small forces is that 'operationally they are not flexible enough to meet all the demands that may be placed upon them, and the help of neighbouring forces may have to be called upon'. In our opinion there can be no objection to help being given by one force to another, and we see no difference in principle between such mutual assistance and the transfer of men or equipment from one division of a large force to another. So far as crime and normal police operations are concerned help is asked for and given without hesitation or formality: we have no record of a request ever having been refused. As regards special occasions, such as royal visits and large demonstrations, most forces never request help, but those forces which have done so include middle-sized and large ones as well as small ones.

17. The second objection of the Commission to small forces is that 'the employment of specialists is difficult and training facilities tend to be inadequate'. The facts show that there is very little difference between the specialists employed in the smallest forces and those between 500 and 1,000 strong. The most commonly quoted example is frogmen, but in fact only a minority of even the larger forces employ these men. True it is that provincial forces can and do seek the help of the metropolitan force in cases of murder and occasionally other serious crimes, but this assistance is properly sought by the large provincial forces as well as the small ones. So far as training is concerned all forces, big and small, send their men and women to the Police College and the district training centres. Some, but by no means all, the forces in the 500 to

1,000 range have their own residential training schools, and places at these schools are offered to forces which do not have them: in this way the latter are under no disability. But the best criterion of training efficiency is perhaps success in the promotion examinations. Results in 1958 and 1959 show that the best results were obtained in forces of 350–499 men; second best, forces from 200–349 men; and, last of five groups, forces of over 1,000 men—the biggest forces of all. The differences are not great but certainly do not bear out the suggestion that 'the optimum size is at least 500'.

18. The third objection is 'promotion tends to stagnate and it is harder than in a larger force for the chief constable to ignore the claims of seniority in filling the vacancies that occur'. In fact, promotion, at any rate up to the rank of inspector, is mainly governed by the ratio of sergeants to constables and inspectors to sergeants, which is much the same in all forces; and variations in length of service before promotion are chiefly due to the policies of individual chief constables and watch committees. In fact the prospects of promotion – sooner or later – are better in the smaller forces than in the larger ones. Of the men who retired in 1959, 1960 and 1961 holding the rank of superintendent or below, only 31 per cent of the men in forces under 200 strong had failed to get promotion, but 47 per cent of men in forces over 1,000 failed to get promotion. The position is that in a small force the odds are seven to three on gaining promotion, whereas in a large force, although promotion may on average come a little earlier, there is little more than an even chance of obtaining it at all.

19. The next objection of the Commission to small forces is that 'discipline is difficult to enforce impartially and unpleasant in its effects because the disciplined man is too well known to his chief constable, to his fellows and to the public'. This is the type of remark which is easy to make but extremely difficult to refute. We have good reason to believe that discipline is in fact better in forces where every man is known to the chief constable and any serious default is likely to come quickly to his personal notice. As far as serious offences are concerned the man will in any event be dismissed from the service.

20. The Commission next say that 'the risk of undesirable pressure being brought to bear on members of the force by local people, whether members of the local authority or others, is greater'. This remark again is not capable of refutation by assembling facts, but it would be just as easy and probably far more true to say that there is less danger in a small force, where every member is known to the chief constable and under constant supervision by senior officers, than where these conditions do not apply. No instance of such undesirable pressure was reported by a single authority to which the questionnaire was sent.

21. Finally the Commission add: 'and not least important it is no easy matter to find for such a [small] force a chief constable with all the qualities which ought to go with that responsible and semi-autonomous office'. The questionnaire asked whether this difficulty had been experienced and in every case the answer was 'No'. Some police authorities emphasized the general high standard of candidates, quoting the names of unsuccessful ones who had later secured appointments elsewhere and subsequently became chief constables of the larger forces in the country or ended their careers as H.M. Inspectors of Constabulary.

22. Further questions elicited that crime detection reaches a higher standard in small than in large towns even when the comparison is between adjacent towns of different sizes.

23. Amalgamation of the smaller borough with county forces would, we are sure, inevitably lead to less efficient policing of these towns. The response to local needs is much more likely to be achieved where the police authority concentrate their interest and attention on the maintenance of law and order in the town than where they are responsible for a wider area. The representatives of one town on a large authority cannot reasonably hope to secure a proper appreciation of its needs. Moreover, the police officers concerned do not have personal local knowledge or bonds of local loyalty.

24. Operational efficiency, too, is higher in towns than in counties, partly because of the more compact area of control and partly because as a matter of fact the ratio of police to public is generally higher in borough police areas than in county police areas. In particular the built-up areas which now fringe most large towns are not always policed to the same standard as the towns themselves where the town has its own police force. If amalgamation were to reduce the standard of service in the towns to that at present given in fringe areas that would be a most retrograde step.

25. Men who live a settled life, frequently buying their own houses and not having to uproot their families and send their children to fresh schools, are likely to be more contented and efficient than men who do not enjoy these advantages. This is evidenced by the fact that far more men apply to transfer from large forces (especially county forces) to small ones, than vice versa.

26. Finally, the police statistics show that the cost per man in county forces is higher than that in borough forces.

27. There are, in fact, probably no two local government services for which the ideal administrative area coincides, and it is therefore unlikely that any local authority area will ever be ideal for the purposes of police administration or for any other single purpose; but if a service is to remain within the local government framework some form of compromise must be struck,

157

perhaps at the expense of marginal administrative efficiency. To suggest that the optimum size of a force is probably 500 or upwards – a proposition which we have sufficiently refuted – is to suggest, as the Commission appreciate, that prima facie only 44 forces out of 158 in Great Britain should be retained as separate entities. There is no 'local government' in an arrangement of this kind. We stand by the view that an authority which is, or is eligible to become, a county borough, must be presumed capable of discharging effectively all the functions of a county borough council. If an authority are entitled to county borough status, they are entitled to maintain their own police force. In recommending that an authority should become a county borough the Local Government Commission must be presumed to have satisfied themselves that the area can be policed efficiently as a separate unit. The Royal Commission recommend that the procedure of inquiries into amalgamation schemes should be altered so as to facilitate the merger of forces. We disagree and are of opinion that the Home Secretary should remain under an obligation to show expressly that greater efficiency would result from amalgamation. . . .

Bibliography

OFFICIAL PUBLICATIONS

Report of the Royal Commission on Police Powers and Procedure (Cmd. 3297, 1929).

Report of the Committee on Police Conditions of Service (Cmd. 7831, 1944).

Report of the Royal Commission on the Police, 1962 (Cmnd. 1728).

Minutes of Evidence given before the Royal Commission on Police 1962 and Memoranda (particularly those submitted by the Home Office (Appendix II), Association of Chief Police Officers (Day 15), Association of Municipal Corporations (Day 11), Professor E. C. S. Wade (Appendix II), and Professor J. D. B. Mitchell (Appendix II)).

Reports from the Select Committee on Estimates and Minutes of Evidence 1957–8 (H.C. 307) *and 1962–3* (H.C. 293).

POLICE INQUIRIES

Inquiry in regard to the interrogation by the Police of Miss Savidge (Cmd. 3147, 1928).

St Helens County Borough Police Force. Reports to the Secretary of State (Cmd. 3103, 1928).

Report of the Tribunal appointed to inquire into the allegation of assault on John Waters (Cmnd. 718, 1959).

Sheffield Police Appeal Inquiry (Cmnd. 2176, 1963).

Report of Inquiry into the Action of the Metropolitan Police in relation to the Case of Mr Herman Woolf (Cmnd. 2319, 1964).

Report of Inquiry into Allegations made by Mr Eric Fletcher, M.P. (Cmnd. 2562, 1964).

Report of Inquiry by Mr W. L. Mars-Jones, Q.C. (Cmnd. 2526, 1964).

DEBATES

On Provincial Police Forces, 1958 (213 House of Lords Deb. col. 4ff.).

On Report of the Royal Commission on Police, 1963 (677 H.C. Deb. 5s. col. 680ff.).

On Police Bill, 1963 (685 H.C. Deb. 5s. col. 81ff.).

Police Bill, 1963 (Standing Committee Debate, Standing Committee D. 3rd Dec. 1963–25th Feb. 1964).

ARTICLES

H. B. SIMPSON. 'The Office of Constable', *English Historical Review*, 1895, p. 625.

HELEN M. CAM. Essay in *The English Government at Work 1327–1336*, Vol. III (on Coroners, Constables and Bailiffs).

N. PARRIS. 'The Home Office and the Provincial Police in England and Wales 1856–1870' (1961), *Public Law*, p. 251.

J. ANDERSON MCLAREN. 'The Police Authorities of the United Kingdom: Their Constitution, Revenue and Responsibility at Law' (1910), 22 *Juridical Review*.

SIR JOHN ANDERSON. 'The Police' (1929), *Public Administration*, p. 192.

J. A. G. GRIFFITH. 'The Control of the Police by Local Authorities', Address to the Annual Police Conference, 1959, published by County Councils and Municipal Corporations Associations.

SIR LEONARD DUNNING. 'Discretion in Prosecution', *Police Journal* (1928), p. 39.

GLANVILLE WILLIAMS. 'Discretion in Prosecuting' (1956), *Criminal Law Review*, p. 222.

B. KEITH-LUCAS and D. N. CHESTER. 'The Independence of Chief Constables' (1960), *Public Administration*, 1.

G. MARSHALL. 'Police Responsibility' (1960), *Public Administration*, 213.

W. T. WELLS. 'Public Control and the Police' (1959), *Political Quarterly*, p. 141.

W. T. WELLS. 'Nottingham – Some Constitutional Reflections', *Justice of the Peace and Local Government Review*, 7 November 1959.

J. D. B. MITCHELL. 'The Constitutional Position of the Police in Scotland' (1962), *Juridical Review*, 1.

JENIFER HART. 'The County and Borough Police Act, 1856' (1956), *Public Administration*, 405.

JENIFER HART. 'Some Reflections on the Report of the Royal Commission on the Police' (1963), *Public Law*, 283.

D. LLOYD. 'The Willink Report' (1962), *Journal of the Society of Public Teachers of Law*, 69.

D. LLOYD. 'Report on the Police' (1962), *Solicitors' Journal*, 677.

D. G. T. WILLIAMS. 'The Police, Public Meetings and Public Order, 1962' (1963), *Criminal Law Review*, 144.

A. W. BRADLEY. 'A Failure of Justice and Defect of Police' (1964), *Cambridge Law Journal*, 83.

FRANK ELMES. 'Complaints against the Police', *Police Review*, 13 March 1964.

H. BERAL and M. SISK. 'The Administration of Complaints by Civilians against the Police' (1964), *72 Harvard Law Review*, 499.

J. GOLDSTEIN. 'Police Discretion not to Enforce the Criminal Process', *69 Yale Law Journal* 543.

I. BROWNLIE. 'Police Questioning, Custody and Caution' (1960), *Criminal Law Review*, 298. (Subsequent articles by Glanville Williams and Christopher Williams.)

L. H. HOFFMAN. 'The Judges' Rules', 7. *The Lawyer* (1964), p. 23.

J. C. SMITH. 'The New Judges' Rules – A Lawyer's View' (1964), *Criminal Law Review*, 176. Further articles, *ibid.*, pp. 154 and 173.

GENERAL WORKS

WILLIAM LAMBARD. *The Duties of Constables, Borsholders, Tything-men etc.* (1602).

FRANCIS BACON. 'The Office of Constables' (1608), *Works*, ed. Spedding and Ellis, 1859, Vol. 7, p. 749.

JOSEPH CHITTY. *A Summary of the Office and Duties of Constables* (3rd ed., 1844).

FREDERICK MAITLAND. *Justice and Police* (1885).

SIR EDWARD TROUP. *The Home Office* (1925).

SIR FRANK NEWSAM. *The Home Office* (1954).

SIR JOHN MOYLAN. *Scotland Yard and the Metropolitan Police* (1934).

W. L. M. LEE. *A History of Police in England* (1901).

MAURICE TOMLIN. *Police and Public* (1936).

CHARLES REITH. *A Short History of the British Police* (1948).

CHARLES REITH. *A New Study of Police History* (1956).

JENIFER HART. *The British Police* (1951).

SIR C. K. ALLEN. *The Queen's Peace* (1953).

L. RADZINOWICZ. *A History of English Criminal Law*, Vol. 3 (1956).

JOHN COATMAN. *Police* (1959).

LORD DEVLIN. *The Criminal Prosecution in England* (1959).

C. H. ROLPH (ed.). *The Police and the Public: An Enquiry* (1963).

HARRY STREET. *Freedom, the Individual and the Law* (1963), Chap. 1.

MARY GRIGG. *The Challenor Case* (1965).

BEN WHITAKER. *The Police* (1964).

MICHAEL BANTON. *The Police and the Community* (1964).

J. LL. J. EDWARDS. *The Law Officers of the Crown* (1964).

GERALD ABRAHAMS. *Police Questioning and the Judges' Rules* (1964).

ASSOCIATION OF MUNICIPAL CORPORATIONS. *City and Borough Police Administration under the Police Act, 1964* (1964).

Works on the history of individual police forces are listed by Henry Parris in Vol. 34 of the *Police Journal*, pp. 286–90.

Index of Cases

163

General Index

165

For Product Safety Concerns and Information please contact our EU
representative GPSR@taylorandfrancis.com
Taylor & Francis Verlag GmbH, Kaufingerstraße 24, 80331 München, Germany

www.ingramcontent.com/pod-product-compliance
Lightning Source LLC
Chambersburg PA
CBHW050518280326
41932CB00014B/2371